PARENTING YOUR ANXIOUS TEEN:

Effective Strategies to Help Your Highly Sensitive Child Cope with Social Stress and Freeing Him From Anxiety, Worry, and Depression

Aurora Morris

© Copyright 2020 - All rights reserved.

The content contained within this book may not be reproduced, duplicated or transmitted without direct written permission from the author or the publisher.

Under no circumstances will any blame or legal responsibility be held against the publisher, or author, for any damages, reparation, or monetary loss due to the information contained within this book. Either directly or indirectly.

Legal Notice:

This book is copyright protected. This book is only for personal use. You cannot amend, distribute, sell, use, quote or paraphrase any part, or the content within this book, without the consent of the author or publisher.

Disclaimer Notice:

Please note the information contained within this document is for educational and entertainment purposes only. All effort has been executed to present accurate, up to date, and reliable, complete information. No warranties of any kind are declared or implied. Readers acknowledge that the author is not engaging in the rendering of legal, financial, medical or professional advice. The content within this book has been derived from various sources. Please consult a licensed professional before attempting any techniques outlined in this book.

By reading this document, the reader agrees that under no circumstances is the author responsible for any losses, direct or indirect, which are incurred as a result of the use of information contained within this document, including, but not limited to, — errors, omissions, or inaccuracies.

"When you're feeling anxious, remember that you're still you. You are not your anxiety."

~Deanne Repich

TABLE OF CONTENTS

INTRODUCTION

When looking at the statistics of anxiety and depressive disorders in children and teenagers, it is reported that seven to fourteen percent of these children will have an episode fueled by intense depression by the time they reach the age of fifteen. Out of a recorded one-hundred thousand adolescent youth, two to three thousand of them will acquire some sort of anxiety or mood disorder. Sadly, out of those thousands, eight to ten of these children will commit suicide.

We live in a world that has evolved into a technology-driven society. Starting at very young ages, we introduce our children to video games, television, and tablets. While some of these things can be educational, they end up being used as a primary means of entertainment with them. Kids are growing up now learning how to be themselves by mimicking what they see on a screen. Their values, how they talk, and how they treat others is based on what they watch on the television or on a video application.

Long gone and in the past are the traditional family dinners that we used to have. Parents sitting around the table with their children, eating a home-cooked meal, and sharing the adventures of their day with one another. Technological advances have completely annihilated the need for meaningful conversations with one another.

Parents talk to their children and teenagers via social media avenues, and that is also how they keep up to date on the things that are going on in their children's lives. Even when phone calls occur, they are usually short or "butt-dialed." The rise in anxiety about talking on the phone has risen because technology has made it possible to talk to each other without actually speaking. We can order our food without talking to an actual person. Everything can be done using online applications.

The problem with all this technology and lack of communication is that there is not a tone to the discussion. Things can be misconstrued in so many ways through a text message or instant messenger conversation, and they usually are. Feelings get hurt when they don't need to be, but when they are, the one who was hurt will keep it to themselves, and it festers causing stress and potentially anxiety toward the situation that was created.

There are so many different things out there that young people have to deal with. Teenagers have so much that they are going through. They go to school. They worry about college, friends, relationships, sports, and what is going on in their home life.

They are the ones who are old enough to know if mom and dad are experiencing money problems, and it can cause them to worry about something; they have no control over. They won't talk about things though because they have been raised in a society that doesn't share feelings, just non-verbal communications.

Teenagers have unrealistic expectations to live up to. This does not necessarily mean they have them at home, but they see social media and all of the posts that are made daily and try to be what they are told they are supposed to be. A lot of anxiety and depressive disorders have low-self esteem as a symptom. This could be helped if we didn't hold ourselves to such high standards that are set online.

As parents, we have loosened up our hold on our children. Children are becoming younger and younger when we begin to make them privy on information that they honestly should know nothing about. Children don't need to know about things that cause adults stress, yes, we are open and honest with them about it. The problem is that our children, at this age, are not mentally mature enough to process this information. We put this stuff on them anyway.

There is the stress of school that we turn a blind eye to as well. Things have changed so much in the education world since we went to school, and even though we used to have our parents help us with our homework because it was all uniformly done, the methods have changed. Things have changed to a common core which is completely different and unfathomable to most of us. We are in a situation where we can't help our children with their homework, so if they don't get it on their own, they get lower grades. Then, when they get these lower grades, we dish out punishments because they aren't living up to their potential and we assume it is because they aren't doing the work.

I don't know about you, but this is a huge dilemma for a teenager. They are supposed to get into a good college, but if the family can't afford to pay for it and they can't get a scholarship, they aren't left with too many options besides something like student loans. They begin college already in debt and worrying about money.

By the time they reach adulthood, they are more than likely already exhibiting serious anxiety disorders and maybe even a depressive disorder. They are more likely to have these if their parents have them too. Then they are hit with a double whammy. People don't like to talk about it though because they feel like it is a sign of weakness.

There are a multitude of anxiety disorders and depressive disorders listed in the chapters that are coming up. They all have symptoms that overlap and some that are distinctive to their respective disorders. A lot of times, it is hard to diagnose these disorders, especially the older you get. By the time a child or teenager reaches adulthood and none of these problems have been addressed, they may feel like they are losing control or going completely insane, which is a sad thing. That is why paying attention to the signs and seeking the help and assistance a child or teenager needs early on is important and will offer the most benefit to them.

Coping with anxiety and depressive disorders can be hard. Finding the right type of therapy or medicinal combination is truly a trial and error system. Most often, people try to combat these things without using medications because a lot of these medications have side effects that make them feel weird. In most instances, a therapist will be the ones who determine the best courses of action. There are a lot of different therapies that can help with anxiety and depression. They can help with working to diminish stressful situations or just to cope with the emotions that come with them. Things like hypnosis, cognitive behavioral therapy, and exposure therapy are highly promoted for people who struggle with stress, anxiety, and depressive disorders.

There are also a lot of things that can be done at home to help your child or teenager and their struggles with stress, anxiety, and depressive disorders. Good communication is key, though. If you can't talk to your child, that is something that will need to be changed before you can make a difference anywhere else. You can't be there friend when dealing with stress, anxiety, and depression. You have to be the parent and make some tough calls that they won't like sometimes.

CHAPTER 1: ANXIETY DISORDERS COMMON IN CHILDREN AND TEENAGERS

Generalized Anxiety Disorder

Generalized anxiety disorder is an anxiety disorder that can present itself a couple of ways in children and teens. It is normal for children and teenagers to show some anxiety regarding new scenarios and people, but if it becomes a persistent problem, it could be an indication of something more severe, like generalized anxiety disorder.

Children and teens who have generalized anxiety disorder show a lot of fear or worries when the situation does not seem to warrant them. Things like future events, being accepted by their friends, performance on their schoolwork, family matters, and their own personal skills may be something that these children seem to worry about without anything to ease their fears. If these worries and fears begin to interfere with their daily functions, it may be time to seek out professional help to get them through it.

Some symptoms that are generally presented when a child or teen is suffering from generalized anxiety disorder are:

- The child or teen worries about things that are beyond their control

- The child or teen fears things that have not happened yet

- The child or teen has constant stomach aches or headaches and don't want to go to school

- The child or teen is unable to relax, even at home in a controlled environment and they seem more irritable than usual

- The child or teen may seem overly clingy toward family members and may have trouble being away from home due to the fear that something bad will happen to them or their parents

Panic Disorder

Panic disorders in children and teens can often be hard to diagnose. While most of the time, a panic attack is usually an indicator of the disorder, it doesn't necessarily have to accompany it all the time. Panic disorders are treatable and if caught early enough, there is usually very little side effect into adulthood.

Panic attacks are scary, especially to a child or teenager. They don't understand completely what is happening to their body, and it can catch them off guard, which typically can make it much worse. The symptoms of a panic attack include:

- Intense fear that something bad is happening or going to happen

- Physically trembling or shaking

- Racing heart or palpitations

- Shortness of breath or the feeling of suffocation

- Sudden dizziness and/or just feeling lightheaded

- The fear that there is a loss of control

- Feeling like things aren't real around them

Panic disorders can become debilitating for children and teens. The symptoms can interfere with their schoolwork, relationships, and normal development. They may begin to avoid certain situations, fearing that they could have a panic attack. If the panic disorder is severe enough, children and teens could develop a condition that is called "agoraphobia." This is when someone shuts themselves up inside their homes, afraid to go outside. Others may be even more susceptible to thoughts of suicide or self-harming habits. There is even an increase in the amount of alcohol and substance abuse among younger adolescents due to the fear of panic.

Separation Anxiety Disorder

Separation anxiety disorder is a normal part of childhood. Children worry about not being with their parents when being dropped off at daycare or school. Most children grow out of it pretty quickly, and the fears they had diminished. For other children and teenagers, they may not be that lucky.

Separation anxiety disorder is something that can linger in a child from younger years up through adolescence if it is not dealt with early on. Sometimes parents may not even notice the signs until it has blossomed into a full-blown disorder. Children and teens with separation anxiety disorder are constantly worried about being away from parents or someone that they are close to. They truly feel like if they are not with their parents or these people that something bad is going to happen.

All children experience different symptoms, but the most common indicators of separation anxiety disorder are:

- Nightmares or terrors that always have a theme of being separated from someone

- Refusing to sleep alone in their own bed

- Refusing to attend school

- Afraid to be alone, even when old enough

- Constant muscle aches, tension, headaches, and/or stomach aches

- Being clingy, constantly

- Severe panic attacks or temper tantrums when separating from a parent

These symptoms are more severe than what your child may have experienced between the ages of eighteen months and three years old. This separation anxiety disorder is severe.

Social Anxiety Disorder

Social anxiety disorder is an anxiety disorder that children and teenagers may deal with well into adulthood and never be diagnosed. This is the third most common mental health disorder among the population, but it is the one that is most ignored. It is ignored because parents and teachers are not educated on the signs and symptoms in regard to children and teens.

Social anxiety disorder is an intense fear or phobia of social settings. These can range from being among groups of people to giving a presentation in public. The common factor is that the fear that presents itself in the mind is much more intense than the situation calls for. The symptoms for this can be different for different age groups.

The symptoms for pre-school aged children are:

- Fearing new places or things

- Being extremely irritable or whining a lot

- Refusing to speak to anyone

- Being overly clingy or freezing in place

All of these could be misdiagnosed in a child this age, that is why it is very rare for a pre-school aged child to be diagnosed.

The symptoms for school-aged children are:

- Fear of being called on in class-this could include being called on to read aloud or answer a question in front of everyone

- Fear of having to speak in front of the class or give an oral presentation

- Fear of athletic activities because of the spectators

- Refusing to have friends over

- Refusing to participate in any kind of school activity

- Not attending birthday parties for other children because they are afraid

- Being unable to talk to other children or teachers

The symptoms of teenagers are:

- Exhibits a lot of nervous habits-nail biting, hair twirling, excessive fidgeting

- Withdraws themselves even more when asked to participate in a group

- Overly quiet

- Keeps head down and arms crossed when walking down hallways

- Constant fear of being humiliated or embarrassed

- Has very few friends

- Avoids group projects

- Avoids talking to people outside of class

- Often sits alone in the library or cafeteria

- Avoids any kind of setting that requires them to be in a group

Teenagers are at the biggest disadvantage when it comes to social anxiety disorder. These are the kids who seem to suffer more in school and often stand out just because of their anxiety. If these symptoms are not managed early on, these teens may end up with depression, suicidal ideations, substance abuse problems, and eating disorders. If they are lucky and those do not happen, they typically carry the same symptoms into adulthood which can make it hard for them to function in work situations.

Selective Mutism

Children and teens who exhibit the inability to speak in certain social circumstances are generally believed to have selective mutism. This is categorized within the umbrella of childhood and adolescent anxiety disorders. This is a disorder that can prevent children from participating in class and even possibly asking for help when they need it.

Coming across as shyness to most, selective mutism is much more than that. Children are more than likely on the social phobia spectrum end of things when it comes to selective mutism. A lot of times, children are diagnosed earlier verses later, but the symptoms become a whole lot more apparent once they are of school age.

Phobias

Phobia is a blanket term that can have multiple layers. Children, teenagers, and even adults live with phobias every day. Phobias are defined as a fear that is persistent and identifiable. They are typically excessively unreasonable and occur when the object or situation in question is presented, or the anticipation of it occurring is imminent.

Common phobias are fearing animals, heights, blood, flying, closed spaces, insects, and death. In order for a phobia to be diagnosed, the fear has to be present for at least six months straight. This is justifying it as a phobia and not as just a fear that will pass with time and tolerance.

All children and teens will experience different symptoms when presented with their phobia, but this is a list of common symptoms associated:

- Intense sweating

- Shortness of breath/trouble breathing

- Chest pain or discomfort

- Increased heart rate and/or palpitations

- Feeling as if they might faint

- Getting chills or hot flashes

- Becoming completely numb to everything

- Begin to choke because they are frozen

Generally, phobias will exhibit symptoms that are panic attacks but much more intense. They are localized occurrences that happen when presented with the target of the phobia.

Obsessive-Compulsive Disorder

Obsessive-compulsive disorder often comes across as excessive worrying in children and teens at first. The current estimation is that one in every two-hundred children and adolescents suffers from obsessive-compulsive disorder.

Obsessive-compulsive disorder isn't just excessive worrying and trying to not worry despite the fact that no matter what they do, they can't stop. These are called obsessions. From these obsessions stem compulsions which are rituals that they feel they must do to stop anything bad from happening.

Some of the most common obsessions that children and teens who suffer from obsessive-compulsive disorder deal with are:

- Fear of being contaminated by something

- Fear of germs

- Use of lucky or fear of unlucky numbers

- The need for everything to be symmetrical or "in its place"

- Religious obsessions

- Fear of contracting an illness

Some of the most common compulsions/rituals in children and teens are:

- Rituals that involve grooming habits like handwashing, brushing teeth, and combing hair

- Rituals that require constantly checking things like appliances to make sure they are off or double and triple-checking homework to make sure it is completed and correct

- Rituals that require the child or teen to repeat certain habits, like going in and out of a door so many times or rewriting things multiple times

- Rituals to help undo contact with "contamination"

- Repetitive touching rituals, usually in even or odd sets

- Hoarding and collecting because they fear getting rid of things

- Adjusting and organizing and then readjusting them and reorganizing

- Cleaning rituals

During the ages of seven and twelve is when most obsessive-compulsive disorder diagnoses are made in children. These are the years where they are naturally learning themselves and will start to exhibit the symptoms. If it is left untreated, obsessive-compulsive disorder can have a huge impact on adulthood.

Posttraumatic Stress Disorder

Posttraumatic stress disorder occurs when something that is traumatic occurs that creates anxiety and stress for the child or teenager that went through it. Sometimes posttraumatic stress disorder happens quickly after the event, but other times it can happen months to years later. It can occur in any age group. This can also have long term effects that can follow a child or teenager into adulthood. Posttraumatic stress disorder can also be accompanied by substance abuse problems, depression, and severe anxiety.

Posttraumatic stress disorder is commonly caused by something that has happened to the child that was extremely traumatic for them; something happened to someone that the child was close to and it affected them, or even something the child has seen that had an impact on them.

Here are some traumatic events that a child or teenager might have encountered that could cause them to have problems with posttraumatic stress disorder:

- Bad accidents that involved some mode of transportation-either the child or teenager was involved or witnessed it happen

- Sometimes in children who are younger, when they have to undergo serious medical treatments, it can cause them to have anxiety problems

- Being bitten by an animal-this can also provoke a phobia to become present

- Natural or manmade disasters

- Being a victim of or witnessing a violent attack

- Abuse-this could be physical, mental, verbal, sexual, bullying

- Being neglected

There are a lot of factors as to how a child will cope with an accident or traumatic event. A lot of it depends on the type of

34

incident, who was involved, how long the incident occurred, and how supportive the family is in helping the child or teenager get through the incident.

Symptoms that the child or teenager might exhibit as part of suffering from posttraumatic stress disorder are:

- Extremely vivid nightmares or memories from the day or event that caused the stress

- Depressed and irritable

- Sleeping problems-too much or too little

- Loss of the ability to show affection

- Become detached from things they once enjoyed doing

- Stay away from places or people who trigger the memories of the trauma

- Have physical ailments like stomach aches or headaches

- Avoid going to school

- Relive the event sometimes for minutes at a time- these flashbacks can be extremely vivid including smelling, tasting, and feeling like they are in the moment all over again

Diagnosing posttraumatic stress disorder early is important. The sooner the symptoms are dealt with, the easier it will be for the child or teenager to handle the situation and it may not give them problems when they reach adulthood.

Facts About Anxiety

- Anxiety disorders are among the most common mental health issues in the United States. It is estimated that 18.1% of adults are diagnosed with it each year.

- Even though anxiety is not curable, it is treatable, but only a little over 35% of those who suffer seek help and treatment options for it.

- People who suffer from anxiety disorders are more likely to seek medical attention and end up in hospitals being treated on the psychiatric wing.

- Generalized anxiety disorder is more prominently diagnosed in women.

- Generalized anxiety disorder is usually accompanied by major depressive disorders.

- Panic disorders are found in over 6 million adults, but women are twice as likely to be diagnosed over their male counterparts.

- It is not uncommon for those who suffer from social anxiety disorder to wait ten or more years before seeking help with the disorder.

- The average age of phobia onset is seven years old.

- Obsessive-compulsive disorder has been found in patients as young as fourteen.

- A third of patients who have been diagnosed with obsessive-compulsive disorder as adults report having started experiencing the symptoms during childhood.

- In anxiety disorders, rape is the most common cause of posttraumatic stress disorder.

- Children who experience sexual assault are more likely to have the onset of posttraumatic stress disorder as an adult.

CHAPTER 2: DEPRESSION AND MOOD DISORDERS COMMON IN CHILDREN AND TEENAGERS

Major Depression

Major depression is a mood disorder that is often referred to as clinical depression. This generally has more than just the normal daily ups and downs, and it is becoming a serious health concern among children and teenagers.

The common risk factors that could trigger bouts of depression are:

- Excessive amounts of stress

- Physical or emotional trauma

- Abuse

- Neglect

- Other disorders that are psychological

- Smoking or substance abuse

- Illness

- Losing someone important

The symptoms of clinical depression manifest themselves differently in every person, but some of the most common symptoms are:

- Constantly feeling sad

- Excessive feelings of guilt

- Low self-esteem

- Lower than normal energy levels

- Trouble sleeping (insomnia or the opposite)

- Changes in eating habits

- Wanting to die

- Suicidal ideations or attempts

- Feeling irritable, hostility, or aggression without a trigger

- Running away from home or threatening to do so

Healthcare providers are the only ones who can truly diagnose a child or teenager with major/clinical depression. There must be a cluster of the above symptoms that are present in the child's behaviors for a period of two-weeks straight.

Persistent Depressive Disorder (Dysthymia)

Persistent depressive disorder, which is also called dysthymia, is a mild form of depression that lingers for a long period of time. This is the most common form of mental health illness in the United States. Among children ages thirteen to eighteen, this and clinical depression are the most commonly diagnosed mental illnesses at around 11%.

For a child or teenager to be diagnosed with persistent depressive disorder, they must exhibit symptoms most days for at least a year. These symptoms generally include appetite changes, sleeping problems, always fatigued, poor concentration, having trouble making decisions, and feeling hopeless most of the time.

If a child or teenager begins to exhibit the following for more than a two-week period, it is important to get them into a healthcare provider to seek some kind of treatment:

- Feelings of sadness and hopelessness

- Constant worrying

- Low-self esteem or being negative about themselves in comparison to others their age

- Sleeping too little or too often

- Sudden withdraw from family and friends with no explanation as to why

- Extreme changes in eating habits

- Being irritable and aggressive with no provocation

- Poor performance in school

- Physical symptoms that become bothersome- headaches, stomach aches, and muscle aches

You need to seek IMMEDIATE medical attention if your child or teenager exhibits the following as these are possible signs of suicidal behaviors:

- Mentions coming up with a plan to die

- Wants to sleep forever or just disappear

- Begins to give away the possessions that they love the most

- Talks about how they won't be around in the near future

- Expresses the desire to just wanting to die

These are all things to take seriously. Suicidal ideations and attempts are a sure sign of a major mental health disorder.

Bipolar Disorder

Bipolar disorder is a mental health disorder that is classified by periods of mania and periods of depression. This used to be called manic depressive disorder. Children through adults both experience periods of mania and depression if they have bipolar disorder. Mania is when the person, whether it is a child or teenager, has a period of feeling "up." The backside of this is the "low," which is when they experience periods of deep depression.

Symptoms of manic episodes can vary from person to person, but a generalized overview of symptoms are:

- Increased energy (this isn't an energy burst; this is something that can last for days followed by a hard crash)

- Unrealistically high self-esteem

- Sleep disturbances (going for days without needing to sleep or feeling tired)

- More talkative than normal

- Easily distracted

- Thinking in fast-forward

- Extreme reckless behavior-drug or alcohol abuse, promiscuity, taking risks that they would not normally take

Symptoms of the low, or the depressive state of bipolar disorder, are:

- Decreased desire in doing anything

- Lack of energy and fatigue

- Major sleeping changes-sleeping too often or too much

- Feeling bored all the time

- Changes in their eating habits

- Sudden changes in their physical health-complaints of headaches, stomach aches, and body aches

- Thinking about death or attempting suicide

Diagnosing bipolar disorder in children and teens is hard to do. It requires a lot of observation on the part of healthcare and mental health provider. The development of bipolar disorder can begin in childhood or adolescence. It is important to seek medical help to determine if it is bipolar disorder and not something that could be more serious.

Disruptive Mood Dysregulation Disorder

Originally children and teenagers who have disruptive mood dysregulation disorder were diagnosed with bipolar disorder. These children and teens did not exhibit all of the symptoms of bipolar disorder, but for lack of better diagnosis, this was their categorization. Since discovering the disruptive mood dysregulation disorder, understanding these children and teenagers has become easier.

Temper tantrums and moodiness are common for children and teenagers, but when it is extreme, it can be indicative of disruptive mood dysregulation disorder. The symptoms that a child or teenager may experience are:

- Temper outbursts that are severe and occur at least three times weekly

- Exhibit a sad, angry, or irritable mood on a daily basis

- Their reactions are larger than the situation warrants

- Trouble functioning at home, school, and in public circumstances

These symptoms are coupled with some criteria that must be met in order to be considered for disruptive mood dysregulation disorder:

- Child has to be at least six years of age to be considered

- Symptoms typically manifest before reaching the age of ten

- The symptoms have to have been present for at least a year

The symptoms of disruptive mood dysregulation disorder can be present in other psychological, anxiety, attention, and depressive disorders that could be a problem for the child or the teenager. The diagnosis should be given by a certified mental healthcare provider.

Premenstrual Dysphoric Disorder

Premenstrual dysphoric disorder is an extreme form of premenstrual syndrome.

This occurs in adolescents to teenage girls and can be experienced up through adulthood. The onset of the menstrual cycle sends a surge of hormones, and the symptoms for premenstrual dysphoric disorder include:

- Extreme moodiness-feeling depressed, anxiety, rage, and irritability that seem to stem from nowhere

- Extreme instances of crying and unexplained emotions

- Overwhelming feelings and feeling like you may not make it

- Being overly sensitive to rejection or what others might think

- Changes with eating habits

- Concentration trouble and struggling to stay on task

- Extreme physical symptoms-bloating, cramping, tenderness in the breasts, exhaustion, and body aches

The onset of these symptoms can begin at any moment after puberty has happened. It often feels like being a different person for most girls who experience it. This is generally diagnosed by a healthcare provider or gynecologist. It is important for girls and teenagers to seek treatment to help with the symptoms of this so that they are able to function a lot better if it happens.

Facts About Depressive and Mood Disorders

- In the course of a year, it is estimated that sixteen million adults will have at least one interaction with a serious bout of depression.

- Depressive and mood disorders are the third leading cause of hospitalization.

- Depression is responsible for causing the disability for Americans who are between the ages of fifteen and forty-four.

- Women have a predisposition to depression. They are seventy percent more likely to get it before a man.

- In adolescents, one in eight have major depression.

- In children, that number is one in thirty-three.

- Suicide risk in teenagers is increased if their depression is not addressed.

- In the elderly, men are more likely to contemplate suicide than women.

- Over fifty percent of those who take care of a family member who is elderly have the symptoms of major depressive issues.

- Sadly, it is more likely that you will get better mental health care if you are Caucasian than if you are of color.

- Depression happens in a third of patients who have cancer.

- Parkinson's patients have a high chance of developing depression.

- Those who struggle with eating disorders typically have an onset of depression.

- Those who deal with substance abuse issues typically suffer from depression.

- In women, depression can increase the risk of breaking bones.

- Women have their own category for depressive disorders, thanks to their anatomy. Postpartum depression, premenstrual depression, and perimenopausal depression can all occur in women.

- Depression is a world issue, not just the United States. Estimated numbers of eight hundred thousand people commit suicide every year across the world.

- In a lot of third world countries, less than ten percent of the people struggling with depressive disorders receive any hope of treatment.

- Mood disorders are generally found to coexist with some type of substance abuse problem.

CHAPTER 3: CONTRIBUTING FACTORS

Biological Factors

There has been evidence that some mental health disorders are associated with nerve cell circuits that link the parts of the brain not functioning properly. It is like a misfire in the brain's communication system, which are called neurotransmitters. These neurotransmitters can be adjusted chemically using medications to try to bring back a balance to their functioning processes.

GENETICS

Genetics are believed to play a large role in the development of mental illnesses. If a parent suffers from a mental illness, it is possible that their child will suffer from it as well. In studies that were done, scientists figured out that major psychiatric disorders do have a component of inheritability.

Major depression, posttraumatic stress disorder, most anxiety disorders, and obsessive-compulsive disorder showed a rate of twenty to forty-five percent heredity. Substance abuse problems like alcoholism and eating disorders showed a rate of fifty to sixty percent heredity. Shockingly, things like schizophrenia, autism spectrum disorder, and bipolar disorder topped the charts at seventy-five percent heredity.

It is unknown which genes are specifically responsible for the development of mental illnesses. Genome mapping is still in its infancy, and there is not enough consistency for it to be easily mapped since a good portion of the cultivation of the genes comes from the environment of the person. The nature aspect of nature versus nurture is only covered by genetics. If there was a way to predict that a child was going to develop a certain anxiety or depressive order, then intense studies of the genes could be done prior to the nurture aspect becoming a factor. Since scientists cannot tell the future, there is no way to create an unbiased testing on the genes. They do believe that it could be a mutation of several genes, not just one specific gene.

The other side of the scientific debate on mental illness and genes is that a person merely inherits the susceptibility for the disease and not the actual disease itself. What this means is that if a child is born to parents who both suffer from anxiety disorders, then it is possible the child itself will be susceptible to anxiety disorders later on in life. Not that they inherited genes that automatically give it to them. This is more of a nurturing aspect.

INFECTIONS OR ILLNESSES

There was a study done in Denmark that links the possibility of childhood illnesses and infections to the increased possibility of developing mental illness. This study covered a seventeen-year span involving hospital records and prescription records. The study was done over such a large span of time so that they could follow children from birth into their teenage years.

What this study found was that there was a higher rate of mental illness or mental health medication being prescribed in children who were hospitalized for an illness or an infection. Taking depression and bipolar disorder out of the running, it increased the risk of being diagnosed to eighty-four percent and the chances of being prescribed mental health medication to forty-two percent.

If the illness or infection didn't require hospitalization and was treated in an outpatient program using antibiotics, antifungals, antivirals, or an antiparasitic medication, it was determined there was a forty percent greater risk of being diagnosed with a mental health disorder. The prescribing of mental health medications were twenty-two percent higher in these children and teenagers.

When they incorporated the nurture aspect of the equation, they included siblings in the study who had an infection to those who did not. The outcome was astonishing. The eighty-four percent rate of mental health issues was reduced to twenty-one percent. The risk of being prescribed a mental health medication dropped to seventeen percent amongst this group. While the numbers did drastically drop, they still did not completely zero out. There is still an increased risk for those who suffer from childhood illness and hospitalization for infection.

Other studies have been done in regard to this same theory. They do believe that a lot of it has to do with the problems that are caused to the immune system and its response when the child develops the infection or illness. The scientists do believe that it is possible that the immune system response could also be what affects the possibility of developing a mental health issue. They are also trying to research the idea that maybe it isn't the illness or the infection, but the pathogen that causes the problem. Either way, there are a plethora of scientists out there working on trying to figure out the conundrum.

There is a pediatric disorder called pediatric autoimmune neuropsychiatric disorder that comes from the streptococcus bacteria. The pediatric autoimmune neuropsychiatric disorder has been linked to a child developing obsessive-compulsive disorder. They are also linking it to other mental illnesses as well.

BRAIN INJURIES OR DEFECTS

There has been a significant link to anxiety and depressive disorders following an injury to the brain. Since the brain is in charge of the complex functions that run not only the body but emotions and thinking capability as well. Any time there is trauma to the delicate brain tissues, it can have effects across the board when it comes to the functionality of the body and emotional center.

The cognitive functions of the brain are what control how the brain thinks. When this is injured, it can lead to a child or teenager having trouble controlling their thoughts, behavior, and how they deal with emotions and stress. The adjustment and coping with this may put additional stressors on the child or teenager, not to mention the parents. Some common outcomes of this are:

- The child or the teen becoming increasingly frustrated and it increases their emotional vulnerability, making them more depressed or anxious in situations

- The stress of frequent doctor and hospital visits may become too much for the child and the parent

- The parent and the child may worry about their future- this includes their educational future as well

- For teenagers, their desire to be independent may be compromised by the parent needing to monitor their actions-this can cause some defiance and make the teenager even more emotionally vulnerable

There is even evidence that incidents that occur while a fetus is still inside its mother can cause mental illness and delay in the child as it develops. The damage doesn't have to be caused by physical trauma; it can be caused by things like delivery and oxygen deprivation.

Family Factors

Even though there is a biological factor that involves the familial genes that are linked to a parent sharing their mental illness with their child, there are other circumstances that can exasperate that situation. As stated, when it comes to the parents having mental illnesses, it is probable that their child will have a mental illness as well. This includes anxiety issues and depressive disorders. The risk is exponentially higher when the parents have one or more disorders too.

Enter the debate of nature versus nurture. Family is a nice medium of both when it comes to describing what influences parents have on their children, especially in the field of mental health. Inconsistencies and an unpredictable home life can create stressors for children and teenagers that can create anxiety and depressive disorders. Some steps that can be taken to help protect children from a household that may be conducive to potential anxiety and depressive disorders are:

- Keeping it out in the open that the parents do have mental illnesses like anxiety or depressive disorders, and it is nobody's fault

- Getting other family members to help out the situation

- Get educated on how to create a more stable environment in the home

- Counseling services for everyone in the household

- Promoting positive self-esteem practices in the home

- Promote a good sense of inner strength within the child or teenager and reinforce them with good coping skills

- Help find a healthy and stable adult to create a relationship and friendship with

- Teach the members of the family how to build meaningful friendships

- Help find the child or teenager productive activities outside of the home so that they are exercising their emotional growth

It is important that if the parents suffer from anxiety or depressive disorders, they seek out social workers who specialize in offering resources to families. These social workers should also pay attention to children and adolescents in the household to see if they may require additional resources or screenings for anxiety and depressive disorders like their parents.

Environmental Factors

Environmental factors are things outside of your body and science that can influence your world. For the purpose of explaining environmental factors that can affect the impact of anxiety and depressive disorders in children and teens, they are broken down into two separate categories. Physical and social.

PHYSICAL ENVIRONMENTAL FACTORS

Physical environmental factors are factors that have the ability to affect a person's biological makeup or neurochemistry which increases their chances of developing anxiety or depressive disorders. As an example, if a person has an inadequate diet. One that is not full of vitamins and balanced nutrition, it may affect how they are physically and mentally because of chemical imbalances that occur. This can make their anxiety and depressive disorders worse.

Besides nutritional factors creating an effect on the body and influencing mental health issues, sleep deprivation can cause a lot of issues on the body. When the body is lacking sleep, a lot of things can occur. Accidents are more likely to happen when you haven't gotten enough sleep. Balance and coordination are limited which can lead to self-injury. Accidents and injuries are things that can cause trauma to your brain or lead you to have problems with posttraumatic stress disorder if the incident is bad enough.

Substance abuse, smoking, pollution, childhood exposure to toxins, and hazardous conditions can have a huge impact on mental health issues, especially in children and teenagers. These different things all have to do with chemicals entering the body and altering how the body responds to outside factors. Things like poisoning from lead paint can lead to a lot of mental illness. Substance abuse, especially while still in the womb, can cause birth defects and greatly impact the probability of a child or teenager ending up with anxiety or depressive disorders.

SOCIAL ENVIRONMENTAL FACTORS

Social environmental factors are factors that refer to racial, relational, ethnic, and socioeconomic topics and how they affect the way the body copes and adjusts to stressful situations. One of the biggest social environmental factors that can create a negative outcome for stressful situations is the lack of a support system to help get through it. This is especially difficult for children and teenagers when they do not have family or friends to support them and their decisions or actions.

Stressful things in someone's life that could be considered a social-environmental factor are social stigmas, abuse, loss of a parent at an early age, being poor, no religious affiliation, and lack of taking care of themselves. These are all things that can become a difficult task without people there who can help you work through it. A lot of us are lucky enough to have people in our lives to help us work through issues of stress, others aren't so lucky and that can lead to serious depressive disorders and anxiety issues.

Even though mental health illnesses like depressive disorders and anxiety can be inherited through genes, the overall health of your body and your surroundings can greatly influence how the body responds to the outside stimuli.

Signs and Impact of Stress

Children and teenagers learn their coping skills by watching those around them. It is important to recognize the signs of stress in children and teenagers because teaching them early in life how to cope with it are techniques that they can carry into adulthood. Stress that goes undealt with can turn into anxiety and depressive disorders. Stress affects every person differently and every age group differently. Knowing these differences can help identify stress before it becomes a major problem later in life.

In toddler and preschool-aged children, the signs of stress come in the form of:

- Being angry, with no real reason

- Changes in eating habits

- Changes in sleeping habits

- A considerable amount of anxiousness that was not there before

- Being irritable

- Reverting back to infant-like behaviors

- Fear of being alone

- Nightmares or terrors

- Crying uncontrollably or not understanding why they are crying

- Trembling because of being frightened

- Complete withdraw

In elementary school-aged children, the signs of stress begin to evolve into other symptoms that can often be mistaken for other disorders. These symptoms are:

- Physical symptoms such as headaches, stomach aches, and muscle aches

- Not trusting anyone that is around them

- Little to no appetite

- Needing to use the bathroom repeatedly

- Trouble sleeping

- Not caring about their schoolwork or their friendships

- Wetting the bed at night

- Feelings of being unloved

- Being withdrawn from everyone and everything in their lives

- Worrying about their future

Preteens and teenagers experiencing stress can often come in a defiant form. They are not necessarily being defiant but trying to cope with the stress that they are feeling. Other symptoms that preteens and teenagers experience thanks to stress in their lives are:

- Feelings of disillusionment

- Low self-esteem

- Physical symptoms in the form of headaches, muscle aches, and stomach aches

- Total distrust for the people and the world around them

- Acts of rebellion at home and at school

- Experience panic attacks

Stress is something that is completely manageable in children and teenagers. Knowing how to identify the signs and helping them develop positive coping techniques is what will carry them into adulthood with tools already set in place to help against anxiety and depressive disorders. It is completely normal for all children, teenagers, and adults to feel and experience stress in their daily lives. What makes a difference is how they tackle the problem.

Begin by looking at how you handle the stress in your life and make sure you are putting positivity out there because the children in your life are watching. They will mimic you and may even learn how they will deal with their future stresses from you. It is important to start showing them how to deal with these things early so that they are not taken off guard and can actually work through the stresses and stressors that will inevitably be introduced in their lives.

HELPING TO REDUCE THE STRESS

Stress is one of those things that can sneak up on any person of any age. It is not gender-specific, nor is it ethnicity-specific. To be blunt, stress happens. It is the move you make next that can define how you cope with it. The same applies to children and especially teenagers. They don't have a set mechanics yet for dealing with these sorts of issues when they arise, so implementing things to help them get through the day is sometimes enough to keep their stress levels to the minimum.

There are not enough hours in the day and we truly believe that if we keep our children and teenagers busy, that will keep them out of trouble. Therein lies the problem. We keep these kids so busy that they don't even have time to think. We see how well they jump back into things after being sick that we use this same mentality when they are exhausted and never stop to think about if they are being overscheduled during the week. Even as adults, there needs to be some downtime in our schedules to be able to bounce back after doing so many activities. If you wrote down your schedule and examined your family interactions, are they always on the go? If they are, then you are probably overscheduling yourself and your family.

Playing is an easy thing for younger children to do. They generally don't think about all the things that we think about and they use their imaginations a lot more than we do. Older kids, especially teenagers, need to have time to simply play. Unprovoked play like riding a bike, going to the park, or anything that is not in the schedule allows for some shedding of stress in the body. This might even work for the overly exerted adult from time to time too.

Make sure you are making sleep a thing of importance. Sleep is an important tool to help minimize stress and we often overlook that fact. This is also another indicator that there is too much going on in the weekly schedule, and if there is not enough sleep during the week grades will eventually suffer. Make sure that bedrooms are conducive to sleep time. There is nothing that says television is good for children, so keep that as well as other electronics out of the bedroom. The bedroom should only be used for sleeping and it will be more productive sleep if there are no distractions.

Pay attention to how your children are acting and teach them to listen to what their body is telling them too. If your child is constantly pushing themselves and are worn down, eventually their body is going to say "enough" and break down on them. Stress will eat away at them especially if they lack sleep and that makes it easier for the body to completely shut down. If your child is irritable, it might mean that they have been pushed to a breaking point, or it could be indicative of something a lot more serious.

Work on your stress while you work on their stress. Seeing you positively dealing with the stress in your life will make your child or teenager want to positively deal with it in their life. This may even help open the doors to communication between the two of you. They may have questions about how you handle stressors in certain situations, and this will give you the opportunity to check in on them and how they are truly doing.

Try to create rituals within your house, routines to help everyone minimize the amount of stress they have when getting ready in the morning or before going to bed. Try to sit down a few times a week in the morning and have breakfast together. If work permits, try to sit down every evening for a family dinner. Institute a family game or movie night. Open up the channels of communication between everyone while seeing each other face to face.

Another way to alleviate the stress of stress is to prepare your children for it. Let your child or teenager (especially the teenager) know that no one does everything perfect one-hundred percent of the time. There is no way that we can all know everything all the time either. Human beings make mistakes, that is just the nature of things. They should learn how to make the right decisions, but honestly, it is just as important for them to be taught how to recover from a bad decision too. We cannot expect a teenager or a child to learn from their mistakes if we aren't teaching them how to. Taking the time to show them where they may have gone wrong is a good way to eliminate the stress in them trying again in the future. Their anxiety might be high in the same situation if they don't know how to fix it if it were to arise again.

CHAPTER 4: HELPING YOUR CHILD

Helping your child or teenager handle their anxiety, stress, and depressive disorders often start at home. You are the first line of defense for your child and are often the first to notice the symptoms they exhibit for these. First and foremost, you have to let your child or teenager know that stress is a completely natural response that the body gives when in a situation with stressors. If they do not feel like they are the only ones dealing with this, it will be easier for them to talk to you openly about it.

Helping Your Child Manage It

As a parent, it is hard for you to watch your child go through something that you have no control over. Anxiety and depressive disorders are out of your control, but you have the ability to help your child understand it and work through some of the symptoms. The first thing you can do for your child is to educate yourself on these disorders. Knowledge is power in these situations. It is not possible to completely understand the inside of your child's mind, but it is possible to be open enough that they can share with you what is going on.

Creating an environment that is low stress can help your child have someplace that they feel safe. Make sure that you are being supportive of your child and listening to them. All your children or teenager want to know is that you are actually listening to them and giving them appropriate attention. By appropriate attention, that means that you are not allowing the negative behaviors, but you are not punishing for them either.

The balance has to be between allowing self-expression under the pretenses that the child is open with you about what they are feeling. Hiding how they feel is only going to make what they are feeling even worse. The concept is to make communication open so that they can tell you about how they are feeling. Letting your child know how you feel too can give them some insight into how you handle the stressors that come along in your life.

If you have to seek outside treatment for your child, make sure that you are promoting it in a positive way. Let your child know and understand that sometimes getting help from a professional is the only way to manage what they are dealing with, and it does not make them weak. It is quite the opposite; it makes them stronger for seeking out help to deal with their emotions and what they are feeling on the inside.

Do Not Avoid It

The worst thing you can do as a parent of a child or teenager who is dealing with anxiety and depressive disorders is to ignore it. Some parents like to pretend that if it does not exist, then it is not a problem, but all it does is make the problem even worse. Sometimes parents just don't recognize the signs, that is not the same thing as avoiding the subject.

It is a possibility that the parent suffers from the same problems that their child is developing, and they have not come to terms yet with what they are dealing with themselves, and this will make it impossible for them to help their child. This makes it hard for the child to learn when the parent is avoiding their own issues.

Facing anxiety and depressive disorders head-on are the best way to learn how to cope and deal with them. Do not allow yourself or your child to avoid situations that have stressors to trigger them. Offer to be next to them to help them get through the situation or talk with them and come up with a plan for when the stressors occur. Most situations are out of our control and when that happens, the best way to cope with them is to have a plan. Make sure that your child knows their action plan and what they need to do in each situation.

Practice with your child so that they can actually utilize the plan. Think of it like the tornado and fire drills that are practiced in schools. If the plans were implemented, but the children didn't practice them, in a time where the actual emergency occurred, no one would know what to do and chaos could occur. The same idea applies to an action plan for stressors. If it is not practiced, it is just a pointless plan.

Create Positive and Realistic Expectations

Too often we have high expectations of our children and when we have those expectations and they can't reach them, they end up depressed or upset with themselves. Work with your child on creating a list of things that they want to accomplish. If they want to get through the day without experiencing a panic attack, help them list positive actions they can take to work toward that. An example of an unrealistic expectation for this would be saying that they are going to cure themselves immediately of having panic attacks.

Keeping the expectations of your child realistic can help them work through the issues that the stressors in their lives cause them. Making sure that they are making positive strides is important too. That is not to say that they are not going to have bad days, even as adults, we have bad days. Linking the bad days to negative expectations can actually make those bad days worse. Despite the bad days, find a way to make something positive out of them.

Respect Their Feelings but Don't Give Their Feelings Power

Children and teenagers want to feel like they have a voice and that they are being heard when they tell you how they feel. There is a difference in giving them respect and letting them have what they want. The same applies to the respect that you want as a parent. You want your children to give you respect, but if you are constantly walking all over your children and making them unhappy, they are not going to respect you as a parent.

Just because your child is having trouble with anxiety or a depressive disorder does not mean that they can have control over everyone else's lives. If your child doesn't like something and it causes them stress or severe anxiety, but everyone else in the house is fine with it, seeking out therapy to help your child get over their fear or learn how to release the stress would be a way to respect that they do have this feeling but you aren't letting it have all the power.

Children have to learn that when something is stressing them or giving them anxiety or fueling a depressive disorder that it is a feeling that is controlling them. By showing them how to respect themselves enough to relinquish that hold over them caused by those feelings, they can begin to work through the emotions and feelings. Your child may have some negative feelings toward you at the beginning of this process. That is only natural. They expect that you will give into them, and that is final, but once they understand why you are fighting so hard for them, they will accept it and the whole situation can become a positive experience for everyone.

Do Not Reinforce Their Fears

At some point in our lives, we have feared something. It could be the dark, clowns, an animal, or even the idea of someone breaking into the house. Whatever the fear is, do not reinforce it. It is okay for you to acknowledge the fear, which is different from reinforcing it.

Here is an example. If your child is afraid of the dark and is having trouble sleeping in their own bed in their own room, offer them some solutions so that you are not sharing a bed with them. This is probably where the negotiations will start because kids are extremely good at negotiating terms. If they want all the lights on in the house at bedtime, you have to explain to them that no one else in the house would be able to sleep under those conditions. Then they will more than likely work down to a hallway light and their bedroom light. Tell them that they are not able to reach their full potential of sleep that they need to be productive in school, and that won't be an option. However, installing a night light in their room is something that is an option. If you stand your ground and acknowledge the fear, they will be more open to your suggestions.

Fears and phobias cause extreme amounts of anxiety in children and teens. Some of them are far more dramatized than they need to be, but you have to understand that to them, it is that intense. Breaking it down for them so that they can see they are in no danger and that fear cannot hurt them in their present situation will help them. You cannot keep them from playing outside because they are afraid of seeing a bug. You cannot keep them from going to the grocery store because they are afraid of large groups of people. Being their pillar of strength in these situations and making them face them will ultimately ease their fears so that one day they can handle it on their own.

Encouraging Tolerance

Children and teenagers don't understand what is happening to them. They feel like their body has betrayed them when they are experiencing stress, anxiety, and depression. They have to be taught how to tolerate these feelings that they are feeling. If they automatically feel like these feelings are the enemy, they may be more likely to try to ignore them until they build up and cause even more damage than if they had just accepted that they exist. The first step for them to do this is you.

People learn how to act from other people. It is a big game of mimicking and especially holds true when children are involved. If you are tolerable of your child's swinging emotions and even of your emotions, your child is going to be able to identify and examine them a lot better. This can also help when you are around people who may not understand what it feels like to have anxiety or depressive disorders.

If your child has a panic attack while out in public with you, and you help them through it by using calming techniques and talking to them, someone may see this and be able to help someone else. There is not a whole lot of tolerance out there when it comes to anxiety and depressive disorders. A lot of people keep it hidden in the dark because they are ashamed, which can make them perceived negatively to some of their peers. Making sure that mental health awareness is a tolerable topic, it can be easier for those who suffer to be open about it.

Keep Anticipation Times Short

Even as an adult, we feel like time passes so slowly when we are anticipating something to happen. This is even more intense for children and teenagers. What may seem like a minute to us could feel like an hour for them if they are worried or anxious about something. Trying to keep the anticipation time as short as possible in these situations is the best idea.

This could be a blessing and a curse given on how your child reacts to different stimuli. In the first scenario, say that your child has a lot of anxiety about going to the dentist. You know that if you tell your child that they are going to the dentist, they will most definitely worry about it until the appointment is over. This worry can cause them to put themselves into a panic and eventually cause a panic attack. Because of this, you choose to wait until you are literally a block away from the dentist's office to tell your child where you are going. This short anticipation time helps them get through the appointment with as little repercussion from their anxiety as possible.

Second scenario, still taking your child to the dentist, only this time you tell your child about it a week in advance. Your child is the type who needs to be able to plan things and get themselves ready for the appointment in order to not worry about it. This is the other side of the anxious child. If this child were surprised spur of the moment with this appointment, they would probably have a panic attack because they did not get a proper planning period.

This is why knowing your child and how they react to stressful and anxiety-filled situations is important for you as a parent. More often than not, you need to keep the times short for a child. They do not process things the same way as an adult, and if they are caught off guard, they are more likely to adapt to the change than to panic.

Talk It Out

Communication with your child or teenager is the easiest way to understand what they are going through. Even if they have not been diagnosed yet, talking with your children on a regular basis may make it easier for you to pick up on the signs of their mood changes or other symptoms that may become even more apparent with conversation. We live in a day where everyone has a social media account, or they use a cell phone and a lot of time, genuine conversations are lost in translation.

Start having conversations with your children and monitor how they are handling stressors like school, friends, relationships, and responsibility at home. Picking up on the subtle hints that they may be giving away even though they don't realize it could be the difference between them fighting their mental health problems alone or with a team behind them. Catching these things early can mean for an earlier diagnosis too.

Come up with a game plan with them when they begin to feel too much stress. Kicking the stress before it turns into harder issues to deal with is important. If you plan to work on coping with stress, it can make for better strategies in adulthood.

Be A Role Model for Handling Things

It has already been stated multiple times that we are an influence on how children and teenagers act in times of stress, anxiety, and depression. A child will not learn good habits during stress if you aren't showing them when you are experiencing it. If something happens and you end up stressed, so you yell or throw something, the only thing you are showing your child is that when they are stressed, they should express it in the same way.

It is inevitable that role models make some poor choices from time to time. Everyone is human and makes mistakes. Being able to express that the mistake was made and being able to work through it with your child, you can teach them how to change the way they process different kinds of stress.

Create A Support System

Everyone has heard the saying, "it takes a village" in reference to the raising of a child. This is especially true when they grow into a teenager. Having a support system in place for a teenager allows them to have the tools they need to be more independent when solving problems. Having this support system also shows them that they have more people out there who love them besides there parents and sometimes all it takes is another person to lean on to solve some of life's biggest problems.

The biggest role model in a teenager's life is their mom or dad. These are the two people that they have looked up to since early childhood. In order for them to see that the functionality of a support system works, you must have one in place for yourself first. Once they see that a support system works and that accepting help is okay, they are more likely to work on building one for themselves, with your help of course. Let your teenager see what it is like when a community of people come together. If there has been a death in the neighborhood, allow your teen to help you prepare a dish to take to the widow or widower and take it to them. Knowing that someone cares about others can let them know that others care about them.

There are many adults in your teenager's life that could be potentially great for their support system. Teachers that they admire and who care a lot about their grades are a good example. If you go to a church that has a youth group, the group leader may be interested in being a part of the support system and offer good insight for your teen. Don't forget that there are some great potential support system members in your own family as well. Grandparents, aunts, uncles, cousins, and other members could be great role models and support systems as well. A lot of time we only see these family members at holidays which makes it more of a formal setting, try to incorporate some of these family members in informal settings as well like game night or a random family dinner.

As a parent, our first reaction when our teenager needs help is to do it for them. This is not something that has changed since they were learning how to walk or when they had their heartbroken for the first time. We have to get out of that habit though. We can no longer jump to their rescue if they have a problem, we must insist that they look into their support system for help with the answer. We can't be next to them during all hours of the day and that is what having the support system is all about. It is okay to even let them make a mistake or two in this journey; they will become better problem solvers and less stressed the next time the same type of problem arises.

Support having your teenager cultivate relationships with other adults who have the same passions as they do. A lot of times we don't always enjoy what our teenager enjoys. Maybe they like to play the guitar, and you fancy the violin. Letting them make friends with a local artist who plays the guitar may be a good way for them to extend their safety net and have people in it who are more like-minded.

Nip Favoritism From the Start

Being the parent of a child who suffers from anxiety and/or depression is already a tough job. What can make it even tougher is when they have a sibling who does not suffer from the same types of thoughts and feelings. Essentially you are put in the middle of a tug-of-war match between the two. Setting some rules from the very beginning might help alleviate some of the discord between the two.

First things first, you have to make sure that both children know that they are loved. That no matter what they think or how they feel, they are the center of your world and there is nothing that could change that. This gets the foundation out there relatively quickly that neither one of them is above the other one in terms of need.

Find time to be with both of them, separately. If your non-anxious child wants to go to the mall shopping, but your anxious child is having a bad day and cannot handle the thought of it, find someone to stay with them or reach out to the support system that is in place so that you can take your other child to the mall to shop. The same goes for the opposite way too. If there is something that your anxious child needs to make them feel comfortable but the other has no desire to participate, don't make them. Letting each one of them know that you can make time for them separately can help keep fighting at bay.

Make sure there is also time for all of you to spend together as a family too. Make a game night; this way you don't have to put the anxious child in a situation that might cause a panic attack, and the other child is still getting quality interaction with everyone. If you do decide to go out, pick a place that everyone enjoys and make sure that everyone understands they are a support system for each other.

The general fight you will see is that the non-anxious child feels like they are not getting to do the things that they want to do because the anxious child is holding them back. That is why finding ways to get them doing what they want separate helps keep them both satisfied in ways that they think they are winning. The truth-Parents: 1 Kids: 0.

Don't Be THAT Parent

It is important to remember that teenagers cannot be handled the same way as you would handle a younger child. Teenagers are a breed all their own. They should not be handled with the same kid gloves that you handled them with since they were infants. Make no mistake, though; if you give them an inch, they will take a mile. There are some important things that you need to remember when you are handling anxiety in a teenager, things that you wouldn't do with a younger child.

You are a good parent. You have read the books, you have done classes, and you have brought up some amazing children over the years. Now you have to deal with a teenager who has a lot of anxiety problems and you want to be the one to make it all go away. Somewhere in that heart of yours, you feel bad for them, like their anxiety is all your fault. Because you feel bad, you want to make it easier on them. They do not want to go to school, so you don't make them go. You enroll them in an online school so that they do not have to face the peers that made them uncomfortable. They are afraid of making mistakes while trying new things, so you allow them to stay in the safe zone and never push them to try new things. Sure, this is like walking on a tight rope, you don't want to push your children too hard, but you don't want to not push them at all. They need to be encouraged and cheered on if they are going to make their place in the world. They cannot get over their anxiety if they never have to deal with it, to begin with.

On the reverse side of things, pushing them to face their anxiety too quickly can backfire in your face and make their anxiety even worse. You need to have that strong hand but soft enough to push them in the right direction, slowly. These are the parents who probably do not have to deal with anxiety on a chronic or daily level. The teenager is not going to work through their anxiety in a night, and the sooner you realize this and help them come up with ways to work through what causes their anxiety, the sooner they are going to realize this too. If you are always just pushing them to face it, they are not going to come to you for help and they may even withdraw from you completely. That is a whole different problem altogether and can lead to issues with depression and possibly suicidal ideations. There is nothing worse for a teenager than to feel like they are alone in this world.

Enter the parent who is an extreme activist for teenage anxiety. These are the parents who feel the need to advocate for their teenager and every other teenager out there with anxiety whom they feel needs a voice. These are the parents that read all the books, take all the classes, and attend every therapy session with their hand in the air. More than likely this is a parent who has been fighting the battle with anxiety for a long time and they don't want their teenager to have to go down that road, so they are on the front line trying to fight the anxiety for them. They mean well, but they are missing the point entirely. This actually can create more anxiety for your teenager, and it can lead to them feeling so overwhelmed that they just give up on trying to work through their own anxiety because you are so focused on your own self-help mission. The thing to remember is that if you want to help your teenager, they need to be in control of the situation. You are simply there in a supporting role for them.

Do not make the mistake of thinking that your child could be lying about their anxiety. While it does happen, it is best to error on the side of caution and try to get treatment and coping strategies for your child. Parents who believe that their child is only manipulating them by creating stories of anxiety tend to retaliate against their teenager with annoyance and disciplinary actions. This will only push your teenager further away from you and more than likely make their anxiety that much worse. Your teenager is so embarrassed to be dealing with the feelings and emotions that are in control of them that if you are in doubt of them, they may start doubting themselves or look for more drastic measures to make their problems go away. This could lead to substance abuse problems and even suicide.

There are often a lot of misconceptions in regard to anxiety, especially in teenagers. Parents don't understand why something can seem so extreme to their teenage child when nothing has happened to them to warrant the feelings that they have. There doesn't have to be a reason for why they feel the way they do. Sometimes there are reasons sure, but most of the time it is just something they have a genetic predisposition to go through. There is no rhyme or reason, but there is the "what happens next" to anxiety in teenagers.

Now that you know that being THAT parent means, how can you avoid being it? Give your teenagers the tools that they need to take on their anxiety on their own. Make sure that they know they can come to you for help and insight, but that you cannot and will not fix it for them. It is a fact that you cannot fix it for them, and they will come to realize this as they learn more about what they are going through, but they have to have this realization on their own terms and in their own time. Do not fall into the guilt-trip that teenagers are so good at pulling either. They may make you feel like you are abandoning them on some deserted island without a canteen, and they will act that way too, especially if you have fought all of their battles for them in the past. Do not let them get to you.

Handling Teenage Depression

If you even suspect that your teenager might be depressed, you need to act on your instincts. Depression is one of those disorders that left untreated can blow up into something even more debilitating. This is not something that will just go away on its own, either. Watching and waiting is never the approach to take when dealing with teenage depression. If you aren't sure that depression is the culprit for your child's mood and personality changes, the best way you can find out is by opening up a line of communication with them. Bring your concerns up to them, but in a non-judgmental way. These teenagers who are going through depression already think poorly of themselves, they may not be able to handle the thought that you are judging them too.

There is a good chance that they aren't going to just come out and say, "yes, I'm depressed." You can leave it open for them though, that you are willing to talk about whatever it is that might be bothering them. Try not to ask them a lot of questions either because this might overwhelm and exasperate the situation. Sometimes opening up communication by getting them a card and leaving it on their desk letting them know you love them and are there to talk whenever they feel ready is all they need to know to take the first step and ask you for your help.

They may not respond to your techniques the first go around. They may be stubborn or just not ready to talk, but make sure you keep trying. Don't be overly pushy about it, because then they will just back away from you even more. Kind of a gentle nudge that lets them know you are still there. Waiting.

When they are ready to talk to you, keep in mind that you are there to listen to them. There are too many times that, as a parent, we hear our teenager say something and our automatic response is to chastise them. Refrain from doing that in this instance. The important part of this is to realize that they are talking to you and this is your chance to help them by listening and only offering up advice or assistance when they prompt you for it.

Remember that you can't fix them. You want to; you are a parent. As a parent, we only want our children to think of gumdrops and rainbows, but sometimes we have to understand that there are going to be some things that rain on their parade and flood them out. You have to make sure that they know you are listening by acknowledging how they feel. There is no point in them communicating with you if you are just going to be a brick wall with nothing to say. It is possible that how they are feeling will be the most ridiculous thing you have ever heard, but it is something that is real to them and it is causing them emotional pain and suffering. The least that you can do is acknowledge it. I am sure if you think back to a time when you were a teenager or young adult, there was something completely outlandish that you ended up feeling depressed or upset about. Your support person probably thought the same things you are thinking right now but they helped you through it by acknowledging that what you were feeling was real.

If all of the above fails and your teenager insists that there is nothing wrong, but you know deep down that there is something wrong. Take it among yourself to reach out to someone else that is in your teenager's life and see if they can get them talking. A lot of times teenagers don't want to disappoint their parents or bother them with something that they feel like the parent is going to find stupid. A teacher or counselor at school might be able to open up an impromptu conversation with your teenager and get them talking without them realizing they are opening up. The whole point is that they need to get it out to someone and if it isn't you, then you need to find the person who can do it.

HELPING YOUR DEPRESSED TEEN

People who are depressed pull away from everyone. Even the ones that they love. Teenagers are no different in this aspect. If a teenager is suffering from depression, and they begin to isolate themselves, this will only make their depression worse. Trying to get them to reconnect with the things they used to enjoy doing is an important step in trying to deal with the depression itself.

If you do suspect that your teenager may be suffering from depression, reflect on how much you have spent talking to them face-to-face. This is something that you need to start doing immediately if you don't do it already. Getting in conversation, not on the phone or through text, is a good way to gauge your teenager's emotions. Simply let them know that you want to be involved and that you want to be there for them. This will do a world of good for them.

Try to get your teenager to engage socially with their friends. Have them plan a get together with their friends, order a pizza, watch a movie. Anything that will get them interacting socially with people and prevent them from closing themselves up in their room. Try getting them to participate in a sport or in a volunteering initiative. That way they feel important and a part of something. Being involved in something can keep them from becoming isolated and dwelling on their depressed feelings. They may also be able to build a wider support system by developing new relationships with people outside of their immediate family.

Make sure that your teenager is making their health a priority. There is a deep connection between mental and physical health. Get your teenager up and moving by exercising with them. Go for a walk together and talk. Anything to stop them from being immobile. It is immobility that allows the depression to fester and being active is a natural antidepressant.

Limit their screen time. Yes, we do this with younger children, but it shouldn't stop just because they have reached their teenage years. Social media is a pariah for negative feelings and gossip. This can influence how your teenager feels about themselves. Too many violent movies or depressing movies can make their feelings even worse. Plus, if they are on a screen, they are not thinking about their health and being active.

Balanced nutrition is as important for mental health as it is for the rest of your body and its systems. Vitamin deficiencies can make depression worse, as can poor nutritional habits. Make eating healthy and being active in a family initiative. This can help you conquer some of your teenager's depression without singling them out as the reason for the food and exercise changes. Make sure that everyone is getting plenty of sleep so that they are metabolizing the nutrients they need and are giving their bodies the time to rejuvenate that they require to function at peak performance.

Know when you cannot help them any further. Seeking professional help is necessary for most circumstances. Having a certified mental healthcare provider who can assess the situation, especially in situations where suicide may be a risk factor, is the best thing that you can do for your teenager. If your teenager is open to receiving help from a professional, do the research together. This is only beneficial to them if they are willing to open up to the professional. It may even take seeing a few different ones before they find the one who makes them feel comfortable enough to open up.

Explore all of the different options when it comes to treating depression in your teenager. Medication should not be the first answer in any situation. Sadly, it is usually the one that is pushed the hardest for parents with teenagers who suffer from depression. Be your teenager's advocate and seek out other treatment options first before going straight for medication. However, in situations where the depression is extreme, it may be necessary to put your teenager on medication. These would be instances where suicidal risks are high.

Know that these types of medications come with risks though. The creation of antidepressants was tested on adult specimens in testing trials, not teenagers. The testing on how it impacts the brains of teenagers or younger has not been substantiated as of yet. There is a concern that certain antidepressants may leave a lasting impact on the development of the brain in these cases.

The impact of brain development is the least of your worries, though when considering an antidepressant for your teenager though. The side effects alone are enough to stress you out as a parent. The very medication that is prescribed to help with depression and suicidal thoughts actually has the side effect of causing suicidal thoughts. Those at higher risk are ones with a family history of bipolar disorder and those who are in the first two months of taking the medication. This is generally how long it takes to develop the medication in your system. If you do decide to go the medicinal route, make sure that you are attending the follow-up visits and monitoring your teenager closely.

BEING SUPPORTIVE OF YOUR DEPRESSED TEEN

The best thing you can do for your teenager while they are going through depression is to simply be supportive of their treatment option. Make sure that they have a say in the way that it is being dealt with too; they are the ones who know their body better than anyone else. Making the decision for them will only make them feel like they are incapable of making decisions and their self-esteem is going to sink even lower making the depression even worse.

Be understanding of what your teenager is going through will help you in the long run. Living with a teenager who is battling depression can be exhausting. The mood swings and the emotions that are flying through the air can make you want to pull your own hair out but understanding that they are not in control of their own mind right now is the best way to help them. Having patience and understanding for them and not making them feel bad about their feelings will take you far.

Make sure that you are staying involved in their treatment plan. That doesn't mean that you have to go into their therapy sessions and sit next to them and listen to the conversation. Usually, most therapists won't allow parents in the sessions but will offer some insight afterward. Follow the advice of the professional seeing your teenager. Let your teenager know that you want to be involved and want to help them get through whatever it is causing them so much pain.

Depression is a marathon; it is not a sprint. Make sure that you are celebrating the small victories. Things like when your teenager invites a friend over to stay the night. They go to the mall and buy themselves something nice to wear to a party. Prepare for the bumps, though. There will be setbacks. It is a fact of life, coming up with a plan for handling these setbacks is what will determine if it is a large setback or a minor one. Patience is key to this race.

TAKING CARE OF YOURSELF AND EVERYONE ELSE

Trying to take care of your teenager that is in the battle against depression can be a time-consuming task. There will be days where you realize that you haven't eaten all day because you were so focused on them that you didn't take the time to check in with yourself. You can't let that happen all the time though. You are of no use to your teenager or your other family members if you aren't taking care of yourself too. Your family depends on you and it is important that you aren't making yourself sick in the process of taking care of everyone else.

In conjunction with your physical health, your mental health is important. You are focusing so hard on helping your teenager that maybe you haven't thought about how you are feeling mentally. Afraid to say the wrong thing, you may be bottling up your emotions. This isn't healthy for you to do. Seek out a support group for the parents of teenagers who are suffering from depression or set yourself up an appointment with your own therapist. Having someone who is an unbiased third party that will listen to you can help you get your frustrations out.

Be open with the family about all of the emotions and depression going around. Keeping the rest of the family in the dark about your teenager and what they are going through is not helping anyone. Make sure that everyone knows to go on as normal; they don't need to tiptoe around any issues trying to avoid upsetting the teenager. Yes, they are emotionally fragile, but this is something that they are working on and will have to learn how to work through real-life situations. We aren't given a name tag in the real world that says, "Hi, my name is Depressed. Don't talk about this or that". That isn't how it works and using kid gloves on the situation only makes it worse.

Get everyone involved in the issue of depression. This is exponentially important if you or your spouse suffer from it because then the children, not just the teenager, are more likely to inherit it. If you do have younger children, getting them involved can help them develop healthy coping strategies that they can use as they get older. Depression doesn't have to be a dirty word in your house. Depression is actually a natural process in the mind, and as long as it is caught before it becomes a major disorder, it is something that we all learn from. There are so many things that we can be depressed about, but it is the coping mechanisms that are developed at a young age that can help well into the teenage years and then eventually into adulthood.

CHAPTER 5: TEENAGE SUICIDE

Suicide is one of those subjects that people like to sweep under the rug and act like it doesn't exist. This is especially true when it comes to teenagers who commit suicide or attempt it. Parents try to turn the attention on to themselves by thinking that they did something wrong, so they show distrust in their teenagers while trying to fix themselves and not addressing that the teenager is actually the one who needs help.

This may not be the majority of circumstances, but as a parent of a teenager who has tried to take their own life, it generally ends up in the question: What did I do wrong? The honest truth is you probably did nothing, literally. There are often signs and symptoms that allude to a possible suicide attempt or even suicidal ideations in a teenager.

The CDC has released the following statistics:

- In suicide attempts, girls are more likely to try and fail to commit suicide. Boys are more likely to die from an attempt.

- In over half of all teenage suicides, guns are the method most commonly used.

Who Are the At-Risk Teens?

Risk factors for the teens who could potentially suffer from suicidal ideations as well as attempts change over time and can vary based on situational factors. The most common things to look for when trying to identify an at-risk teen is:

- Problems with substance abuse-these are often recurrent problems with one or more factors involved

- Impulsive and erratic behaviors with little to no regard for the safety of themselves

- Major influential life changes-being bullied, losing a parent, losing someone close to them

- Family history with a predisposition of mental illness or a history of suicide in the family

- Victim of violence-abuse that was caused sexually, physically, mentally, emotionally, or verbally

- Previously failed suicide attempts

- Easily accessible access to a gun in the home

- Status as a juvenile delinquent and incarceration

- Exposure to suicide-This can be a familial exposure, media, fictional books

What to Look for in a Suicidal Teenager

Teenagers who are at risk of committing suicide often make their intentions known ahead of time. These cries for help generally get overlooked though. If a parent has never had to deal with these sorts of thoughts or feelings, it is possible that they aren't going to recognize the signs.

Teenagers who are contemplating taking their own lives often show a lot of signs prior to actually doing it. They want, deep down, for someone to intervene. Knowing what to look for is important.

Changes in eating or sleeping habits.

If there are sudden changes in the way your teenager Is eating or sleeping, it can be an indicator of something serious, not just suicide. Often times when our bodies are stressed, they will compensate by overeating or not eating seeking comfort. That same principle applies to sleeping. A teen may start to sleep too much or too little, determined by their own body's response.

Loss of interest and withdraw.

Teenagers, especially ones who were active within social circles or in sports that lose their interest and pull away from everything that once brought them joy in their lives, could be showing warning signs of something much worse. Giving up on things that once brought them happiness or staying away from people and places that they used to enjoy can show signs that they are detaching from their world.

Unnecessary risks and acting out.

If ever there was an indicator of a cry for help, this is the one. Teenagers who were never really risk-takers or go from being meek to getting in trouble or throwing childish fits could be trying to tell you something more than you realize. These teenagers often go from being the quiet kid in the back of the room to being expelled for getting into fights. They don't feel like they have anything left to lose.

Substance abuse problems.

It is not unheard of for a teenager to sneak into their parent's liquor cabinets or for them to experiment with things like marijuana and other party drugs. We would like to stop this from happening and we would like to think that it doesn't happen, not with our child. The truth is most teenagers experiment with something. That is not unnatural. What is unnatural is when it becomes a repeated offense. When you go to pour some vodka only to find out that the bottle is now ninety percent water. You go to your medicine cabinet to take prescription pain medicine for your chronic back pain and the bottle is missing. These are the circumstances that need to be monitored. This is especially true in a teenager who has never shown any signs of using before.

Losing interest in school and lack of focus.

This is especially true if your teenager goes from being an honor student to failing their classes. It is understandable that high school is hard and if your classes aren't challenging enough you may lose focus or get poor grades due to not being able to keep up, but if you notice your teenager is just not caring about their schoolwork and they are no longer making an effort, it might be time to do some research on what their underlying causes are.

Sudden obsession with death and dying.

In some ways, this is a natural thing for teenagers and even children. A pet dies or someone else the family knows dies and they begin to wonder about death. Once their curiosity has been satisfied, they move on to the other questions that generally annoy us. It is when the fascination doesn't fade, or they begin making plans for when they die that you should put yourself on high alert.

Verbal cues.

Take special note of the things your teenager is saying and doing that might indicate they plan on committing suicide.

Things like giving away their personal belongings, especially things that are extremely important to them, can be an indicator. They may even imply that they won't be around much longer for you to have to deal with. They may even write notes that indicate their reason and suicide. One other indicator that could be a false negative, but still should make you suspicious is when they have been depressed for a period of time and then bounce back with an overly cheerful attitude. This could indicate that they are planning something, and it has brought them immense happiness.

Diagnosis and Treatment

A lot of the symptoms that have been mentioned could truly be from other health issues that your teenager is experiencing. The first thing you should do if you even suspect that they may be planning suicide is taking them to a healthcare professional. Their doctor is going to be your first line of defense when it comes to figuring out if there is some other underlying mental illness to blame for the changes in their behavior. They should never be left alone if you suspect suicidal ideations.

Teenagers who have a suicide attempt on their medical record should get physically examined by a healthcare provider to make sure that no long term damage has been done. This is also a way to monitor their progress after the attempt. It may require some sort of hospitalization if the teenager seems eager to try again.

Treatment options vary based on age and symptoms. The severity of their condition is also a determining factor. Understand that treatment will start with the days leading up to the attempt and can be very personal and revealing. It is important to understand what brought them to actually trying to end their lives. There is a chance that multiple types of therapy will be involved in the process. Individual sessions between the therapist and the teenager, group sessions between a teenager and others in their similar situation, family therapy sessions, and other therapy treatments as deemed necessary by a mental health professional.

If it is felt that your teenager is still a danger to themselves or that they need the added supervision during the time they are working on their feelings, it may be recommended that your teenager stays in a hospitalized setting. This isn't to make them feel bad about their actions; it is simply to help supply a safe environment where they can get the necessary help that they need. Most hospital settings aren't like what they show in the movies. They are generally an entire floor where there is a common room where the occupants can spend their time as long as they aren't in therapy. Generally, patients can have visitors as long as it doesn't affect their therapy schedules.

How Can I Help Prevent Teen Suicide?

The best way to help prevent teenage suicide is to educate yourself and your teenager. You would be surprised at how often another teenager may be able to help a friend stop thinking about committing suicide. Make sure that there are open lines of communication between you and your teenager as well. Make sure that they know that they can come to you with ANYTHING. There are also additional steps that can be taken:

- Keep prescribed medicines out of the reach of children and teenagers. Don't let them know where you put them either. If they are thinking about suicide, and they have access to medications that could be dangerous, they will consider this a viable option.

- If you have firearms in your home, make sure that they are unloaded and locked up. Have a separate place that the ammunition is locked up too. This is important if you suspect your teenager may be thinking about suicide.

- Get them the help that they need. This should be the first thing a parent does if they think that their child may have a problem mentally.

- Don't over criticize or make your teenager feel bad about the feelings they are having. They have about as much control over their feelings as you do with them.

- Always be supportive. If that means that you attend therapy sessions with them, or you go to a support group for teenage suicide. Do it. They may seem annoyed with your actions at first, but the truth is they need you.

- Make sure you aren't ignoring the initial signs of depression.

  o Teenagers who show signs of depression often start with feelings of sadness, hopelessness, and loneliness.

  o Their performance in school rapidly declines.

  o No interest in doing the things that once brought them happiness.

  o Changes in their eating and sleeping habits.

  o Always seem like they are on edge, agitated, or angry.

If you have educated your teenager on the signs of suicide, they may be able to save another teenager from trying to kill themselves. Teenagers are more likely to recognize these signs before anyone else because even though they may not act upon them, they have probably thought about it at least one time in their high school career.

- Teenagers who hear their friends or other teenagers talking about suicide or showing behavior that implies it should use their intuition and report it. This includes hunches. Their observation could save someone's life.

- Teenagers can offer to go with their friends or the other teen to seek help from someone of authority.

- Make sure that your teenager knows that no matter what, they need to talk to an adult if they suspect that another teenager is going to try to commit suicide or if they are having ideations of doing so. If that adult doesn't take them seriously, they need to keep trying until someone else does.

When to Call A Doctor and How to Handle the Appointment

The sooner you call a doctor about how your teenager has changed and the suspicion that they may be thinking about suicide the better. Doctors are not going to fault you for making appointments where mental health may be a factor. They want your teenager safe just as much as you do. It is definitely time to call the doctor when you notice these symptoms:

- Your teenager is showing signs of extreme depression. They are fearful and anxious more so than usual. They are going to show signs of anger. These will all be out of character for them.

- Your teenager expresses that they feel like they are out of control. This can be a sign of serious mental health conditions and should not be taken lightly.

- If your teenager expresses that they are hearing and seeing things that no one else around them sees or hears, it is important to get them to the doctor. These hallucinations could be a sign of substance abuse or a psychiatric condition. Often times, the teenager may believe what the voices they hear are saying and this can cause them to cause harm to themselves.

- If the changes in their eating and sleeping pattern has them going three or more days without eating or sleeping, this can be a serious sign of illness. They are going to need immediate medical attention because, without sleep or energy in the form of food, their bodies will begin to decline.

- When your family members or friends start coming to you with concern about the actions and behavior of your teenager, it may be time to take them for medical attention. Sometimes as parents, we don't necessarily see what others see, so getting that other point of view may save their life.

When you do take your teenager to the doctor, you want to get the most out of this appointment. It is only a waste of time if you are not prepared and able to defend your teenager if it becomes necessary. Parents are their child's first advocates. This doesn't change just because they have begun to grow up.

Before the visit happens.

Before you even get to the appointment, know what you are looking for. Make a list of questions and know what you want the outcome of the appointment to be. This can be as simple as a referral to a licensed therapist.

During the visit.

Make sure to take ample notes. Most doctors are only in the room for a specific period of time and a lot of the time they ramble through what they say to you. Make sure you are taking down what the diagnosis is, what treatments they recommend, and any instructions that they have for home.

If they request any tests or procedures, make sure that you are asking questions about them. Make sure that you understand why they are doing it and the information they hope to obtain from doing it.

See if there are possible alternative treatments out there for the diagnosis. It is your right to know all of the ways that your teenager can be treated. You are not obligated to go with the first method that the doctor throws at you.

If there is a follow-up appointment, make sure you take note of the date and time. Ask the doctor's office if there is an after-hours number where you can contact them if something happens. This is especially important if you are seeking advice regarding their mental health.

After the visit.

Make sure that you are following through with the plans made during the doctor's visit. If therapy was recommended, stay on top of the office diligently until they make the appointment referral. Know your rights when it comes to the healthcare and mental wellbeing of your child. Do not let any doctor walk all over you or tell you how you specifically have to handle things.

If you are ever worried that your child or teenager is going to commit suicide and you find evidence of a plan, a note, or a means of executing a plan, call 911.

CHAPTER 6: THERAPY TECHNIQUES

The first choice for outside help for children and teenagers is usually in the form of therapy practices. Medication is and should never be the first choice by a medical professional since medications for these kinds of disorders are made with adults in mind. Parents often reach out to mental health professionals to look for alternative forms of medication and therapy to deal with anxiety and depressive orders.

Cognitive Behavioral Therapy

Cognitive-behavioral therapy is a type of therapy that focuses on helping someone understand the relationships that are linked between their thoughts, behaviors, and feelings. This is often used to help patients identify and change patterns in their lives that are disruptive.

The basic principle of cognitive behavioral therapy is that there is a link between our thoughts affecting our feelings, which then affects our behavior. The purpose is to identify this before it becomes a problem and shutting it down. By identifying that initial thought in the link, actions can be taken to turn it from negative to positive which then makes the link and chain reaction positive.

HOW COGNITIVE BEHAVIORAL THERAPY WORKS

Cognitive-behavioral therapy is best executed by a therapist who has training in this specific type of therapy. The reason for this is because teenagers tend to look at themselves through a distorted lens, handing the way that they see themselves can be a heavy issue. A good therapist trained in cognitive behavioral therapy is able to help the teen identify those distortions in their view of themselves and teach them how to modify them.

Teens have a way of taking these distorted views of themselves and make them manifest into feelings that are not even there. If someone believes that they don't look the way they should, they feel like everyone is staring at them when reality they aren't. So, the goal of the cognitive-behavioral therapist is to help the teenager identify these distortions and unhealthy feelings at their inception so that they can deal with them before they cause unwanted anxiety or depression.

Once the teenager has fully grasped the distortions in their initial line of thought, the therapist can help them begin learning techniques that help them change their line of thought. By identifying the thought patterns that become associated with distorted thoughts, they can then learn to cope and deal with the underlying issues that they create.

BENEFITS OF COGNITIVE BEHAVIORAL THERAPY

Cognitive-behavioral therapy is a means to teach teenagers how to interpret their environmental surroundings differently. Unlike other therapeutic approaches, cognitive behavioral therapy is a short-term therapeutic approach.

A lot of the time, since cognitive behavioral therapy is linked to the individual problems and how to handle them, so it is more likely that this type of therapy won't try to bring up things from the teenager's childhood.

This type of therapy can help a teenager in other areas of their development, especially if their thought patterns make it hard for them to function in social settings. Cognitive-behavioral therapy can help your teenager:

- With the improvement of communication skills, especially with other people

- Reduce the anxiety that is brought on by specific fears and phobias

- Change their thought processes that can lead to potentially life-threatening behaviors like self-harm

- Change the negative thought patterns that are causing them to have the anxiety and depression

- Increase self-esteem, especially if the teenager has a negative outlook about themselves

- Find positive responses to handling the stress and stressors that occur in their lives

Play Therapy

Another viable therapy option that doesn't necessarily allow the teenager to realize that they are being in a therapy session is play therapy. Play therapy can be used in anyone from the age of a small child through the adult years. A lot of times we only think about children playing and never entertain the fact that maybe letting go and having a little fun ourselves can be a therapeutic act in itself.

Often times when teenagers are put into a talk therapy situation, they are intimidated by the setting. They are stuck between the mind of a child and the mind of an adult and just talking on-demand can be a hard task for them. Sometimes lightening the mood and making it less formal can make it easier for a teenager to open up.

Play therapy is responsible for helping teenagers discover more about themselves and how to handle their emotions, it makes them more confident, and more mature. Play therapy gives teenagers a safe space to express themselves and utilize their creativity while opening up.

Ways to use play therapy with teenaged patients include:

- Playing ball or cards while talking about how the day has gone

- Playing board games and discussing feelings

- Drawing a picture or making a collage to express yourself or your fears

- Sharing songs that help communicate your feelings

- Using clay or playdough to make a model

Play therapy can often help children and teenagers express some of the feelings that they hold inside that they don't know how to express in normal circumstances.

Exposure Therapy

Exposure therapy is a behavioral therapy technique that is generally used for anxiety disorders and phobias. Exposure therapy is generally a longer-term therapy technique. Keep in mind that exposure therapy may not be for every teenager and should be explored prior to choosing it as a course of treatment.

Exposure therapy is executed on the principle of conditioning the body to become comfortable with the stressor that causes anxiety or phobia. After prolonged conditioning, the theory is that it will no longer cause the anxiety associated with it. Exposure therapy is often effective if it is administered by a professional who is trained in this sort of therapy.

There are three types of exposure therapy techniques. The first one is referred to as the "real life" therapy. This type is the therapy that slowly works the patient up to facing the stressor or phobia in a real-life setting. An example would be someone who has panic attacks due to a specific animal. The therapist will set up a safe scenario where the patient will work up to facing that fear until they can be in the same room and even touch the animal without it causing panic or fear.

The second type of exposure therapy is image therapy. The therapist will have the patient imagine the scenario in their mind that causes them the most anxiety and stress. They will spend a lot of time visualizing until their symptoms subside and they can face the real situation.

The third type of exposure therapy is interoceptive. This is where the patient will have to experience and face bodily responses to stress and anxiety learning how to cope with them when the onset comes on.

All three therapies can be clustered together for a patient, or they can be practiced individually. The importance of exposure therapy is that the patient realizes that they are always in a safe space and the environment is controlled. The only time that this will change is when the therapist believes that the patient is ready to take further steps and even then, they will be with them while they experience the exposure techniques. The idea is for the patient to work up to being able to handle the anxiety and the stress on their own.

Hypnosis (Hypnotherapy)

Hypnosis, also known as hypnotherapy, uses techniques in guided relaxation, deep concentration, and attention focusing on helping reach a heightened state of mind which is often referred to as a trance. This is accomplished with the help of a trained therapist. Usually, the therapist will be a trained hypnotherapist.

Hypnosis is usually used in conjunction with another type of therapy, like talk therapy. Hypnosis allows for therapy patients to explore the deeply implanted feelings, memories, and thoughts that are painful for them. It also allows for the patient to uncover things that they have been mentally blocking out. Hypnosis is generally used in two ways. One helps the therapist decide a course of action and the suggestion of rectifying behaviors and the other helps the therapist analyze the patient.

Suggestion therapy utilizes the hypnotic state of mind to make the person more susceptible to suggestions made during that state. This is a type of hypnotherapy that can be good for patients who are in pain or are wanting to kick a habit. This can also help with the way patients perceive certain stressors. During the hypnotic state, the therapist will keep suggesting to the patient that the stressor, habit, or pain is not a problem. That those things have no hold on them. Over time the patient will change their mindset to believe these things.

Using hypnosis to analyze the patient puts the patient in such a relaxed state that the therapist can dig deep into their subconscious and see what might be causing their disorder or their anxious symptoms. This is used especially when it is a traumatic event that may have caused the symptoms and it has been mentally blocked and hidden in the mind of the patient. Once the trauma has been revealed, other methods of therapy can be used to help the patient work through it.

Hypnotherapy is best used when in conjunction with another sort of therapeutic method. The success when dealing with fear, phobias, anxiety, sleeping disorders, depression, posttraumatic stress disorder, stress, loss, and grief can be increased when using hypnotherapy alongside traditional therapy like psychotherapy and talk therapy. Hypnosis has also proven to be a good method for those who need to kick a bad habit like smoking or when symptoms are so severe that they need a method of crisis management.

There are some drawbacks to using hypnotherapy. It is not near as effective in those patients who are suffering from psychotic symptoms like hallucinations. It is considered less effective than medication and treatments for those who do suffer from psychotic disorders.

Because of the leading questions and suggestions by the therapist that are unintended, hypnotherapy is no longer considered a form of mainstream therapy. The accuracy of the patient's memories while under hypnosis could be skewed from the actual occurrence due to the fact that memories fade, and sometimes in their place, we create other ones. Although it is not necessarily a therapy that would benefit everyone, using it in certain circumstances is actually beneficial.

There is no danger in trying hypnosis. The only thing that is a potential drawback is the fact that false memories could be created. Other than that, there is a negative popularity for hypnosis because of those who like to put on shows making people think that someone can hypnotize them to do embarrassing things. That is not hypnotherapy.

Psychotherapy

Psychotherapy is an umbrella term that is used to describe talk therapy with a qualified therapist for a wide range of diseases and disorders. During psychotherapy sessions, the therapist will teach you about the condition you suffer from along with helping with understanding the moods, feelings, thoughts, and behaviors that are associated with it. Methods learned in psychotherapy sessions help you take ahold of your life. This is important in teenage patients because they may not understand what they are going through and doing this will help them understand and take charge.

Psychotherapy can help with a number of disorders that can cause a lot of strain mentally, especially on teenagers. Most teenagers don't understand what is happening to them when they suffer from a mental disorder and generally have no coping mechanisms. Psychotherapy helps a teenager develop the techniques they need to handle their mental disorders.

Common disorders treated using psychotherapy techniques:

- Anxiety disorders like obsessive-compulsive disorder, posttraumatic stress disorder, panic disorders, and phobias

- Major and mild depressive disorders including bipolar disorder

- Therapies for addictions to drugs, gambling, and alcohol

- Anorexia, bulimia, and other eating disorders

- Borderline personality disorder and other personality disorders

- Psychotic disorders like schizophrenia that cause the patient to become withdrawn from reality

You don't have to be diagnosed with an actual disease or disorder to benefit from psychotherapy, in fact, there are a lot of times that underlying disorders go undiagnosed or are not prevalent enough to warrant being diagnosed with the actual disorder. Life has a multitude of stressors and using psychotherapy can help a person learn how to cope with them.

Conflict resolution between a patient and another person, whether that relationship is romantic or simply just an interaction with a colleague or friend. Psychotherapy can help you work through the issues that you are faced when trying to handle conflict in these types of situations.

Many times, our lives and work lives cause us major amounts of stress that lead to high levels of anxiety. This anxiety can disrupt the flow of daily life and cause problems at work. Using psychotherapy to alleviate the anxiety that those stressors can put on these situations is often one of the most common reasons for using it.

Changes in our lives, especially the lives of teenagers, can be a hard pill to swallow for anyone. It doesn't matter if you think that you have your life together or not, sudden changes can cause major disruptions in our chemical makeup. Things like divorces, financial burdens, and death are often stressors that can cause extreme uproar in our lives. Knowing how to work through them is often the best way to manage the stress that they cause. Therapists use psychotherapy techniques to help patients in these situations.

A lot of times we exhibit behaviors that are caused by stressors and we don't realize it. Things like road rage are just natural responses our body personally has to a stressor while driving a car. Psychotherapy can help a patient learn to manage these unhealthy reactions that occur when faced with stressors that trigger them. Controlling the emotions our body uses as defense mechanisms is something that can be controlled even though it isn't something that we think about.

People go through difficult things, not all of us, but some of us experience things beyond our control and have no idea how to work through these. Health issues that are chronic and aren't going to just go away like diabetes, cancer, or the diagnosis of a degenerative disease can often cause depression and a lack of hope. Using psychotherapy as a way to work through figuring out how you feel about this and how to move forward in the future can help reduce the risk of major depressive disorders later on. This is also the same concept of why people are recommended to support groups if they have been diagnosed because seeing others handling the stress of it can help them deal with the realization of it as well.

Traumatic events in our past and even our present can take a toll on our mind and body. Any sort of abuse, sexual, mental, physical, can play a huge part in how we handle future issues that may arise in our lives. Witnessing violent acts or being a part of a violent act can destroy a person as much as being abused can. While it will never heal the damage that has been done, psychotherapy can help with moving forward and learning how to take all of the negative energy and turn it into positive coping mechanisms.

Sometimes the biggest physical symptom that someone may encounter due to stress building up in their life is problems sleeping. They may begin sleeping too much or sleeping too little. Either way neither is a healthy way to cope. Finding healthier ways to cope is part of seeing a therapist. Their expertise is what will make finding solutions easier than on your own.

LENGTH OF PSYCHOTHERAPY AND THE RESULTS

Every person is different. The number of sessions that will be required with a psychotherapist is not an exact science, nor is the guarantee that it will solve all of your problems. Psychotherapy is not a means to cure you or make the feelings you have go away; it is a means of teaching you how to cope with them and how to make the most of your ability to do so in a healthy way.

The number of sessions that you will need with a therapist is going to depend on certain factors that revolve around why you are seeking them in the first place. Your particular illness or disorder will play a huge role in the amount of time you need the therapy. If it is a chronic situation, plan on having more sessions that if it is mild. The types of symptoms you experience and how they affect your daily life will be thrown into the mix too. If these symptoms make it hard for you to get up in the morning or function in a social setting, more therapy may be needed. The other part of this is how well you are responding to the treatment that the therapist has been providing in ratio to the stress that you experience. Sadly, another factor that will determine the length of therapy is your insurance and copay. Most insurance companies have a limit on the number of therapy sessions that they will pay for, so this is something for you and your therapist to keep in mind when planning what you want to work on during sessions.

The entire purpose of psychotherapy is to offer you healthy ways to cope with the things that bring you stress or cause you to have severe depression or anxiety. If you want to see real results, there are a few things you must make sure that you are doing.

Make sure you are seeing a therapist that works for you.

Often times when we see a therapist for the first time, and we give them our history, we stick to stay with that therapist because going through the mental and medical history is such a long and exhaustive process. When we stick to this therapist and find out that we aren't necessarily comfortable with them, we don't get the results that we need. If you don't feel like your therapist is a good fit for your needs, it is okay for you to try another one. Keep trying until you find the one that you are most comfortable with because getting the full results relies solely on how open and honest you are with the therapist.

Think of your therapy journey as a partnership.

Therapy isn't exactly a solo sport. When you are working with a therapist, you need to make sure you are actively engaged in the decision-making process. You and your therapist need to be making decisions together on what techniques you want to try to work through your stressors.

Don't hold anything back.

You have chosen therapy for a reason. The only way it is going to benefit and work for you is if you are open and honest. The same applies if you are choosing therapy for a teenager. They have to be open and honest if they are looking to gain the most from the experience. If you are worried that the emotions or things you need to talk about may offend or you are afraid of your therapist's reactions, talk to them about it. They may be able to put you at ease, and you can open up.

Follow the plan and do the homework.

The worst thing you can do while seeing a therapist is not put what you work on to work outside of the office. Skipping sessions can interrupt the progress that has been made, so make sure you are going to all of the sessions and make sure that you come to them knowing what you want to say if you are feeling discouraged. Your therapist will probably also assign "homework" between sessions. These usually consist of exercises like journaling or writing down your feelings when the stressor causes extreme anxiety. Make sure you are doing this and bringing them to your sessions.

Don't expect things to be resolved instantly.

The biggest mistake made among those attending therapy is that they expect the results to be instantly noticeable. This isn't the case. Most psychotherapy sessions take a little while before even the slightest results are seen. If you feel like it is not working, though, talk to your therapist. They may try a different approach or recommend someone else who they think can help you and your circumstances better.

CHAPTER 7: RELAXATION THERAPIES

Relaxation therapies have become one of the most practiced methods of therapy in recent years. The all-natural approach and techniques that help us manage our own bodies is something that is more appealing than taking medication that can change the very personality of who we are. Most relaxation therapies can be done on your own or in a class setting. There are plenty of videos on the internet that can show you the proper techniques as well. Even if you are trying medications or are following a therapy plan with a professional, learning relaxation techniques on your own can still be beneficial. Overall, calmness is often a side effect of these therapies and when added to a plan already being implemented, it can make the results even more satisfying.

Deep Breathing Techniques

Breathing is a powerful tool if you suffer from anxiety or depression. Sometimes these techniques, when used over time, can help you become calmer and less anxious. Most breathing exercises only take up to ten minutes and require very little preparation. The thing to remember is that the shallower your breath the more anxious it can make you. Following through with learning how to deep breathe can help bring your anxiety down.

To begin learning to use deep breathing techniques, you need to find someplace comfortable. Finding the right place to be comfortable makes all the difference between deep breathing being successful. You can choose to lie on your back in your bed or sit in a chair with your feet flat on the ground. The most important part of this is finding that sweet spot for you to be most comfortable. Once you find this spot, it is time to start the breathing process.

- Start by breathing in through your nose. Let the air fill up your belly and push it outward.

- Once your belly is full of air, breathe out slowly through your nose.

- Monitor to see if you are breathing properly. Put one hand on your belly and the other on your chest. Keep the pattern of breathing in through your nose and filling your belly and letting it out through your nose. The idea here is that the hand on your belly should be moving more than the one on your chest if you are breathing correctly.

- Take three more breaths that are full and deep. Breathe fully and exhale so that you feel your belly moving in and out.

FOCUSING YOUR BREATH WHILE DEEP BREATHING

Using focusing techniques while you are executing deep breathing exercises can help you relax into it even more.

- Begin by closing your eyes and allowing yourself to relax into your breaths.

- Continue taking full and deep breaths. Allowing them to flow in and out deeply but naturally.

- When you are ready, breathe in and imagine that you are filling your body with all of the peace and calm vibrations. Try to sink into this feeling with your whole body.

- While you are breathing out, imagine that all the air exiting your body is the negative vibrations in your life. This can be your stress or anxiety.

- The next time you breathe in, try saying a word or phrase in your head to describe the image. "Calm" or "Peace" can often help strengthen the imagery of the peace and calm you are imagining while breathing in.

- As you breathe out to repeat this same idea, only replacing the positive with the negative vibrations you are breathing out.

- Do this for at least ten minutes.

LEARNING HOW TO INCREASE BREATHS

One important thing about using breathing techniques is learning how to build upon the skills that you learn in order to make these exercises more effective. Learning how to increase the length of the breaths that you are breathing in and out can help you breathe even deeper. The deeper the breath, the more relaxing it will be for you. Shorter breaths are equal to more anxiety.

Increasing your breaths is a gradual process and should not cause you any strain. If you feel like you are straining yourself, you need to slow down and not try to increase so quickly.

While you are in your comfortable position, breathe in and count to five in your head. As you breathe out count to five again. Keep doing this until you are confident that you are able to do this effortlessly.

For the last couple of minutes, try increasing the number by one. If you can sufficiently breathe without straining yourself, the next time you start your exercises, do a few with the lower number and then increase to the larger number.

By the time you have practiced your breathing exercises for some period of time, you should be able to make it to a count of ten relatively easy.

BREATHING AND MUSCLE REACTIONS

Using different muscle groups during breathing techniques can be beneficial because it allows the body to sink deeper into a relaxed state.

To achieve this, as you breathe in, tighten a group of muscles. For example, tighten the muscles in your feet as you take in a deep breath. Hold this tension in the muscles for as long as you hold the breath. As you let the breath out, slowly let the tension out of your muscles as well. This will bring a relaxing effect to them. Repeat this with other muscle groups during your breathing exercises. Work your way all the way from your feet to the top of your head. By the end of your breathing exercises, your body, as a whole, should feel more relaxed.

Meditation

Meditation is used to train the mind to become relaxed and essentially empty from all the anxiety and stress that we fill it with on a daily basis. We cannot make these things disappear completely, but we can reach a point where we can simply meditate and clear it from our minds so that when we revisit the issue or stressor, we can use a different approach. There are several different ways to meditate and several different types of meditation. These can range from beginner to expert.

BASIC CONCENTRATION FORM OF MEDITATION

Basic meditation generally revolves around picking one thing to concentrate on. This is the best form of meditation to start with after you have mastered using the deep breathing techniques. The focal point of the meditation can be on the breathing that you are doing.

The reason that this is the basic form of meditation is that it helps build the basic fundamentals for you to learn other forms of meditation. Learning how to focus on one thing and clearing your mind of everything but that one thing is the fundamental basic principle of meditation. When starting out learning meditation, it is impossible for a person to sit for long periods of time and meditate like those who have been practicing for many years. Slow and steady wins the race.

The benefits of mastering this form of meditation can cause an involuntary response by the body to relax which can prove to be very beneficial.

- Relaxation from a meditative state can help reduce blood pressure

- It helps improve the blood circulation in the body

- Lowers the heart rate and respiratory rate in the body

- Lower levels of perspiration

- Less anxiety and less stress (kind of the point in this scenario)

- More feelings of being well and healthy

LOVING-KINDNESS MEDITATION

The goal of loving-kindness meditation is to create an attitude that promotes love and kindness to everyone and everything around us. This even means enemies. While breathing, the point is to open not only the mind but the heart into receiving and sending love and compassion. Often this is paired with mantras that promote love and kindness.

Loving-kindness can help those who are afflicted by anger, resentment, conflict, and frustration. It helps with creating more positive emotions to help with anxiety and depressive disorders, especially posttraumatic stress disorder.

BODY SCANNING

This type of meditation allows a person to stop and truly evaluate what is going on with them. The idea is to identify the key areas where stress lingers within their bodies.

Starting with the feet, the person will do their deep breathing exercises and focus only on the feet and releasing tension that dwells within them. From there, they will work their way upward until they reach their head.

This is to promote a deeply relaxed state within the body. It is often used by people at bedtime to help them sleep.

ZEN

The Zen type of meditation is derived from Buddhist practices. Those who practice Zen typically practice under a teacher because the different postures and steps are hard to master without someone already skilled in the art. This is a lot like mindfulness meditation. However, there is more discipline to it and it also requires looking at things spiritually.

TRANSCENDENTAL

The art of transcendental meditation is a more spiritual form. It requires the person who is doing it to relax and breathe to a point where they feel like they are transcending above their present state. This is generally practiced under a teacher, and they are the ones who choose the mantra for the session. A lot of factors are considered like birthdate when choosing these mantras. Most people who successfully practice transcendental meditation report feeling heightened mindfulness and spiritual awakening.

Mindfulness

Mindfulness is a form of meditation that also offers other benefits besides those that are included with meditation. The idea with mindfulness is that it exercises the mind to be able to be completely present, aware, less reactive, and not overwhelmed by the situations around us. Being mindful is something that we all do on a regular basis without realizing it, but by practicing it daily, it can be more easily available for us to utilize in situations that may make us stressed or anxious.

Much like meditation, mindfulness is something that has to be practiced. We do already have mindful tendencies; we just need to tap into those. The way we do this is by practicing.

THE BASICS ON TUNING INTO MINDFULNESS

The point of tuning into mindfulness is to help ourselves put some distance between our emotions and our reactions to those emotions. Using the basics and building upon them, like in meditation, can help build a strong foundation for further mindfulness techniques.

Make the time.

You don't need anything special to practice mindfulness. There is no equipment that can make it become easier. There is not a special cushion to sit on. All you need is yourself and set aside time to spend with yourself without heavy distraction.

Examine the moment as it is.

The idea is not to completely eliminate our surroundings or our feelings that we are feeling at the time we are practicing our mindfulness techniques. The idea is to acknowledge the moment for everything that it is made up of, but not allowing judgment to be placed upon the moment.

Let all judgment fade away.

The hardest part of mindfulness is not allowing ourselves to dwell on the judgments that we have hardwired into our brains. Acknowledge it and let it pass on by. There is no room for it, and it is not necessary in the present moment.

Always return.

While it is important to let those distractions and judgments wander way from our mind, we oftentimes find our actual mind wandering away from the point of the mindfulness exercise. If you find this happening to yourself, just bring it back in.

Be kind to yourself.

It is important to remember that there is no exact science to practicing mindfulness. The point is to acknowledge and let things go during that moment without judging the feelings. If you find yourself wandering off the path or find yourself slipping up and judging the thoughts, simply draw yourself back in. You don't have to make yourself feel bad about this either. Be kind to yourself and don't judge yourself either.

Mindfulness exercises are generally simple exercises. They are not necessarily easy, though, especially at first. Don't give up though because like learning any new skill, it only gets better every time you practice it.

WHY ARE THESE GOOD FOR ANXIOUS TEENAGERS?

Breathing exercises, meditation, and mindfulness are all great options for your anxious teenager. These are things that do not take up a lot of time and it is something that they can do on their own or include you in on it. These also teach teenagers that they can help regulate their own bodies and emotions by using things that they are already doing, just with more discipline.

Teenagers are typically embarrassed to have problems with depression or anxiety, but using these techniques; they can do it in the privacy of their own rooms without their friends knowing. They can work on finding their center and when they master the skills, they will feel a sense of accomplishment which helps with their self-esteem.

Exercising

One of the things that tend to plague teenagers the most is their self-esteem. They care about how they look, and they care a lot about what other people and peers think of them. This causes some serious anxiety for them. One way that they can work through this anxiety and their self-esteem at the same time is by using exercise as a form of relief.

Even though there are many reasons to exercise to improve your health, it isn't talked about how it affects you mentally most of the time. By exercising a lot of the physical symptoms like feeling tired all the time, muscle pain and tension, feelings of anger or hostility, and overall mood can be alleviated by exercising. The use of exercising as an outlet for depression and anxiety has had multiple proven effects on the body. With the natural energy boost and increased confidence, it should be one of the first things tried with an anxious teen.

So, what happens to your teenager's mind and body if they are exercising on a regular basis?

Natural antidepressant.

Cortisol is one of those hormones that can cause depression in a body. If your teenager is exercising, they are releasing endorphins, which are the "happy" hormones and they fight off the negativity caused by the cortisol. This helps boost the mood without the use of medications.

It supplies a distraction.

Sometimes teenagers just need a way to escape from all of the things going on in their lives. The same thing can be said for adults too. Exercising gives a means of escape from the current moment and allows you to focus solely on that without worrying about something you have no control over.

Confidence booster.

Exercise can help you lose some of the extra weight or help you maintain your current weight. Teenagers have all kinds of body issues, so if they are exercising in a healthy way, they can feel more confident about themselves and their bodies. This helps them with their self-image and makes them feel so much better about themselves which reduces anxiety and depression.

Social networking.

Exercising can be a whole different kind of social networking. Teenagers spend so much time on social media or on their phones and screens that they lose a lot of human interaction with other people. Exercising, either outdoors or in a gym setting, can help them connect with like-minded individuals. They may even find a whole new support system.

Physical health means mental health.

Stress can actually cause a body to have a lower response to infections which can cause someone under large amounts of stress to be sick more often than those who are not under large amounts of stress. Exercise can help reduce stress on the body and in turn, helps with the immune system response. Basically, being physically healthy can help you be mentally healthy.

Exercising combats stress at the core.

Since exercising can help with evening out the hormones in the body that cause depression, it is simple enough to think that when the endorphins are pumping that it will help eliminate the negative responses to stress as well. Exercise can help head stress off before it truly manifests. Having the hormones balanced from the beginning can make for easier stress management skills.

There are so many different types of exercise activities that a person can partake in. In the beginning, it might be beneficial to consider your level of activity. If you have never run for more than a block, it might not be wise to take on a marathon fresh out of the gate. Make some exercise goals and then make a plan that will help reach those goals.

As a parent, getting your teenager active might be a bit of a challenge at first. They may have even taken their cues from you and that is why they allow the stress and anxiety to overrun their lives. They don't feel like you care about yours, so they don't care about theirs. Now is the time to make a change and doing it together can help motivate both of you.

There are all kinds of exercises that can be done. Some of the best exercises to do for the reduction of stress and anxiety are aerobics, walking, running, tai chi, and yoga. Coming up with a plan for this is always a good idea, so it is running it by your healthcare provider. Mixing and matching these activities are a good idea too because then you won't get too bored. It will keep things fun and new.

Tips for coming up with an effective exercising plan:

Know your limits.

When you are getting an exercise plan together, the first thing you need to think about is how active you currently are at this present moment. Make realistic plans because if you or your teenager try to take on too much and do not accomplish it, that is actually harming your state of mind instead of helping it. Take the slow and steady-state of mind in making an exercise routine. Taking on too much too soon can make for injury as well.

Commit to your plan.

Make a commitment to stick to your exercise plan. If you are helping your teenager with their plan, make sure they stick to it as well. Often times we give up when things get too hard and that feeling of accomplishment goes away with it. Try to take on the plan with the mindset that this is the most important thing that you or your teenager can do for yourselves.

Understand the changes in motivation.

Over the course of your exercise plan, you may find yourself slipping to stay on course. A lot of times it is the monotony of the exercise routine that can drag out and we become unmotivated to keep doing it. When you start to feel like this is beginning to occur, it is okay to readdress the plan you created and freshen it up. Maybe the exercises you chose have gotten so easy that you are bored with them, then now would be the time to go to the next experience level for it. Make sure going into the plan that you understand you need to be able to identify when it is time for it to change.

Keep it fresh.

There is nothing worse than being bored. Our mental health suffers extensively when we are not stimulated mentally. This is important if you take nothing else from the exercise section, take this: **Keep changing what you are doing.** It is a simple thing, sure, but a lot of people fear change. So, they stay on the same path despite the mental turmoil it puts them in. Allowing yourself to change something as little as your exercise routine can start putting you in the position of being able to accept other changes in your life.

Using Aerobic Exercise to Relieve Anxiety

Aerobic exercise is just a fancy term to say "cardio." Aerobic exercises are meant to get your heart pumping. This can be anything from taking a brisk walk, to jump roping, or even dancing. As long as you get your heart rate up from the normal resting rate.

It is these exercises that really get the endorphins going. The blood is circulating; the cortisol is getting itself annihilated by the endorphins and mood begins to improve. It isn't an instant kind of effect. Getting into a good aerobic routine, though can help get the body back on the right path to mental healthiness.

Using Yoga to Relieve Anxiety

Yoga is a type of holistic exercise program. Holistic means that it is centered on the well-being of the whole body, not just one specific area. There is an abundance of poses in yoga that can help with the reduction of anxiety. The point to the poses is to help with relaxation and centering one's mind. Yoga is also a great vessel for working on meditation or mindfulness while using the poses. Remember never to strain your muscles to accomplish a pose. Straining the muscles completely defeats the purpose of relaxation.

USING POSES TO CENTER

Grabbing Toe Pose

1. While standing in an upright position with your feet parallel and about a half-foot apart, tense the muscle in the front of the thigh so that it lifts your kneecaps slightly upward. While keeping your legs straight, blow out a breath and bend so that you are parallel to the ground, with your head and torso moving as if they were one.

2. Continue with the bend and hook your pointer and middle fingers around your big toe and second toe. Grab ahold of the big toe and use your thumb to anchor down the two fingers so that they do not move.

3. As you breathe in, try to lift your trunk as if you were trying to stand back up and straighten your elbows. Depending on how flexible you are, your lower back may feel as though it has hollowed out some. While you are doing this and exhaling, tilt your lower trunk (under your belly button) toward the pelvic bone while releasing the tension on the hamstring muscles.

4. Lift your head and sternum as high as you can without straining yourself. If you strain in this step, then the entire point of the pose is null. Make sure you are keeping your forehead in a relaxed neutral state.

5. Repeat step three for a few breaths.

6. Let the breath out and bring out your elbows, pulling up on the toes and lengthening your trunk. Lower your body into more of a bend.

7. Bring your forehead as close to your shins as long as it remains comfortable. There is no benefit to the hamstrings if you overextend yourself or hurt your back.

8. Hold the pose for a minute. Release the toes and bring your hands to your hips. Raise your trunk as one unit upward.

Angle Pose (Bound Position)

1. Sit on the floor with your legs in front of you. While letting a breath out, bring your heels toward your inner thighs. Drop your knees toward the floor while the bottom of your feet is touching.

2. Bring your feet as close to your body as you can, making sure to remain comfortable. Depending on your flexibility, grab ahold of your big toes or on to your ankles, whichever is easier. Make sure the outside of the feet remains flat on the floor.

3. Try to sit with the hips as open as possible. To accomplish this, relax at the hip bones; your knees should reactively follow allowing them to drop closer to the floor. Sit with your back straight and your shoulder blades squared.

4. Make sure to focus on your breathing and stay in this pose for as long as it is comfortable, with the maximum allotment of five minutes. When the time is up taking a deep breath in and raise the knees from the ground. Exhale and return to the original sitting position with your legs in front of you.

Kitty Cat Pose

1. Get down on the floor with your hands and knees placed equal distance on the floor. (Look like you are crawling) Let your head remain in a relaxed position with your eyes able to stare at the floor.

2. Let out a deep breath and arch your back toward the ceiling. This should feel like someone has taken a rope and tied it around your midsection, and they are pulling it downward. Allow your head to naturally fall but don't force it so far down that your chin hits your chest.

3. As you inhale, go back to the neutral position, number 1.

Moo Cow Pose

1. Get down on the floor like you did with the kitty cat pose. These are often done one right after the other.

2. Bring in a deep breath and arch your back upward. This should feel like someone has tied a rope around your midsection, and they are pulling it upward toward the ceiling. Allow your head to naturally rise and your chin jut outward.

3. As you let the breath out, return to the neutral position you started with.

Tai Chi

Tai chi was originally created by the Chinese as a form of self-defense but has evolved into something more graceful. It is a form of exercise in its evolved form. This is often used as a form of stress reduction and helps with anxiety. Basically, in an easy explanation, tai chi is a series of movements that are flowing and connected that are performed while using meditation and deep breathing.

After learning how to do tai chi correctly and practicing it regularly, it can have an overall positive impact on your health. Tai chi helps with health issues like:

- Decreasing stress

- Decreasing anxiety

- Decreasing depression

- Mood improvement

- Increases flexibility

- Increases energy and stamina

- Helps with sleep quality

- Lowers blood pressure

- Helps with joint pain

Warming Up

Like every other exercise, it is important to warm up before doing it. To do a warmup in tai chi, stand with your feet on the floor with a width between them that is a little bit wider than your hips.

Let your arms relax at your sides and rotate your hips back and forth from left to right. Keep doing this for a few minutes until you feel like your body has limbered up some. You can include rotating your neck and shoulders to include an overall warmup feeling.

Simple Sky Touch Exercise

1. Find a comfortable chair to sit in.

2. Let your hands fall into your lap face up with the fingers pointing at each other. (Like spinning in ballet, only your hands are in your lap)

3. Take a deep breath in while raising your hands to chest level. Turn them outward and lift them above your head.

4. Keep the elbows slightly bent and completely relaxed.

5. Letting the breath out, let your arms fall to your side. Then return them to the normal position from the beginning of the exercise.

6. Do this in sets of ten.

The Windmill

1. This exercise requires you to stand with your feet flat on the floor with a width between them that is slightly larger than shoulder width.

2. Let your body relax, especially the shoulder area, and let your arms fall to your sides limply. Let your hands come up toward your body and your fingers pointing toward the floor.

3. As you breathe in, raise your arms higher toward the center of the body and bring them over your head with your fingers following the point as they go. Stretch toward the sky as you arch your back a little.

4. Let the breath out and bring your body back toward the floor in front of you. Bend at the hip relaxed and allow the arms to hang in front of your body.

5. Breathe in and return to the initial position.

Exercising the Hands

1. Stand with your feet a little more than shoulder-width apart.

2. Bring your arms up to the front of your body and hold them straight out. Keep your elbows, wrists, and hands parallel and straight.

3. Flex your hands to the left using a circular motion at the wrist. Repeat to the right.

Writing Therapy Options

For a lot of people, it is hard to talk out loud about what stresses us or causes us anxiety. For teenagers, it is even harder. While there are so many options available to help with expressing anxiety and feelings, one of the best ways for some teenagers can be using writing as a form of therapy.

Using pen and paper can be an effective form of therapy, it allows for the feelings and thoughts to flow out without being cut off or interrupted. A lot of therapists require their patients to use a journal to record their feelings between sessions so that they can review what happened between them. Doing this on a personal level is no different. Even if you are writing down your thoughts and feelings for your therapist, it doesn't mean that you can't have a separate journal for yourself that you don't have to share with anyone else.

Making lists can also be an effective form of therapy for some patients. Especially those who suffer from obsessive-compulsive disorder, lists are comforting. There are journals that are known as listing journals which is for the sole purpose of making lists. It can be a grocery list. A list of things in a cabinet. A list of things to do the next day. Whatever the list may be, it can be written for therapeutic reasons.

Writing stories, fiction or non-fiction, can be a great way to get feelings out there on paper in a way that doesn't feel like oversharing. Some situations are hard, especially for teenagers who have been through a traumatic experience but writing about the experience and having it happen to someone else can help a teen detach from the situation and see it from another perspective.

Letter writing is another way for a teenager to express how they are feeling. Communication can be hard, especially when there are strong feelings in the way. Writing a letter to someone can help with the communication struggle and let them know what they are feeling. Try having your teenager write you a letter telling you what they are feeling. Now, I know old fashioned pen and paper may be out of the question these days, but sending an email is just as effective. There is also the symbolism of writing a physical letter. Writing a letter to someone who has caused trauma or emotional pain and then ripping it up or burning it can often bring just as much relief as giving it to the person.

Art: Drawing, Painting, Clay Modeling

Art is often a form of expression that allows creativity to flow through a person without limitations. Sometimes it is hard to put feelings into words, but it is easier to express them via color or some kind of painting. You don't have to be an artist by trade to benefit from art as a form of therapy. Using art simply gets the feelings out in the open without having to give a whole lot of back story.

Using methods like drawing and painting can open up a new venue for people who can't really talk about what is causing them so much anxiety. Art can form a distraction and allow for teenagers and other patients to slip away from their reality for a little while when it becomes too much to handle.

Music

Music can be good therapy for teenagers. Picking out songs that help them express their feelings. Using songs to say what they need to say. Even just finding music that effectively describes their mood when they have no words to put with it.

This doesn't have to be limited to listening to music. Playing music can have the same effects as listening to it. Playing the drums, releasing the built-up stress that is causing anxiety and tension in your body. Belting out notes at the top of your lungs and throwing all the pain you feel into the microphone.

Using music to dance can not only reduce stress but be a form of exercise. As you already learned, exercise, especially cardio, releases endorphins and endorphins make us happier. A mixture of all three could be a triple threat to anxiety.

Hot Bath and Essential Oils for Relaxation

Sometimes the simplest relaxation technique is the easiest. There is nothing like a hot bath and a nice bath bomb to make you feel at ease. There is something about the use of aromatherapy oils in a bath that can make someone's muscles completely relax and bring complete ease upon them.

Even just using essential oils outside of a bath setting can help in daily situations. There are so many different kinds of herbs and scents that can bring a natural calming effect. It is at least worth exploring those options prior to taking a pharmaceutical route.

CHAPTER 8: MEDICINAL THERAPY

There comes a point when cases of anxiety and depression can become too much to handle, and medicinal intervention may become required. There are two options when trying to figure out how to manage the symptoms of anxiety and depression and those are natural and pharmaceutical. Sometimes depression can be caused by a chemical imbalance in the brain's chemistry and requires medication to help even it out.

Natural Medicinal Therapies

Herbs have been used for thousands of years and used to treat hundreds of ailments all throughout history. Herbs are the main component in essential oils and can be taken via tincture or supplement form when taken internally. Keep in mind that although herbs are the safest form of medicine, they can carry some real consequences too if they are abused. The best way to learn about proper dosage and what one is right for you is to speak to an herbalist.

Lavender

Lavender is one of the best herbs for acute and chronic cases of anxiety. There are supplements with lavender as the primary base that, if taken before bedtime on a regular basis, have shown the same effects of benzodiazepines which are generally prescribed pharmaceutically for the same disorders. The difference is that lavender doesn't hold the potential risk of dependency that the pharmaceuticals do.

Lavender oil in a diffuser or applied topically can be good for creating a calming environment. Oils used topically can be used to get through acute anxiety situations. Lavender can also be used in teas and create a calming effect, especially when used in conjunction with other herbs of the same category.

Turmeric and Curcumin

For a long time, turmeric was an herbal remedy for problems with inflammation and digestion, but it has recently been discovered that it is extremely beneficial in cases of depression and anxiety. Curcumin is the active ingredient in turmeric that helps act as an anti-inflammatory and has been recently studied for its effects in reducing symptoms of anxiety that have been brought on by chronic stress.

The general method of taking these is through ingestion. There are supplements available with recommended dosing

155

instructions already on the bottle. Some people prefer to get raw form or powder and add it to smoothies. Turmeric is often used in cooking, but when cooking with it, that isn't really the preferred method to get the amount that it would take to help with anti-anxiety effects.

Reishi

Reishi is an adaptogen that helps the mind adapt to the stressors in life instead of constantly feeling like it must be in fight or flight mode. They are capable of keeping stress-regulated using a tonic type of action on the adrenal glands which produce the chemicals in our body that support fight or flight. This is most commonly in the form of a mushroom; it is still medicinal, though. It is one of the best things for anxiety because it creates a calming effect. It is also used for anxiety that prevents someone from sleeping.

Ashwagandha

Another herbal remedy from the adaptogen family is used to help with anxiety and has been shown to reduce cortisol levels, which essentially resets the body's response to stress. This may help reverse the predisposition of anxiety. This can be taken in pill form, tincture, or even by ingesting. This is good for right before bed because it helps shut down the worrying part of the brain.

Chamomile

Chamomile is probably the most renowned poster herb for stress reduction. When it is used on a regular basis, whether in a tea, capsule, or supplemental form, it can greatly reduce the existence of daily stress, which reduces the anxiety factor as well.

Lemon Balm

In western Europe, lemon balm has been dubbed the "gladdening herb." This is because the effects of the herb seem to make one brighter. This has been used for hundreds of years, much like lavender. It is known for increasing calmness and decreasing anxiety; however, this is not an herbal that you want to consume or take in the morning. It Is known to have a sedative-like effect which can hinder your alertness. It is best to take this in the evening before bed.

Chasteberry

Sometimes anxiety for a girl or woman only seems to flare up during the premenstrual time. Chasteberry, also known as vital, has been shown in studies to help the levels of anxiety that come during times of PMS. It helps with not only the anxiety but the depression that can come along with it during this time.

Kava kava

Kava kava is a good emergency solution for panic attacks and for bouts of anxiety that are sporadic. It is important to work with a professional when experimenting with this because there is a heightened risk of liver damage associated with it. It is available in capsule form, but for a quicker response from it, using a tincture is recommended. Start off with a low dose because it can be overwhelming. Gradually work up in dosage until you find the one that works the best for you.

St. John's Wort

St. John's Wort has been used for a very long time in the treatment of mental illness. It is best associated with treating depression. In a study, it was found that this herbal medicine had more of an effect than a placebo and was almost as good as taking pharmaceutical medication for depression. It has shown more results in mild cases of depression and is not recommended for moderate to severe forms.

Ginseng

Ginseng has been used in traditional Chinese medicine to treat stress and depression for many years. They believe that it increases mental clarity and energy, both of which suffer when a patient is suffering from depression.

Pharmaceuticals

There are many manmade drugs that exist for the treatment of anxiety and depressive disorders. Most of them are not safe for children and teenagers because when they are chemically composed, they are made for adults to take. It is always best to talk to your healthcare provider to find out what the best option is for you and your child.

Selective Serotonin Reuptake Inhibitors (SSRI)

Selective serotonin reuptake inhibitors are generally prescribed for moderate to severe depression symptoms. These are safer than other types of antidepressants and cause the least amount of side effects.

- Celexa (citalopram)

- Prozac (fluoxetine)

- Lexapro (escitalopram oxalate)

- Paxil (paroxetine HRI)

- Luvox (fluvoxamine)

- Zoloft (sertraline)

Selective Serotonin and Norepinephrine Reuptake Inhibitors (SNRI)

Selective serotonin and norepinephrine reuptake inhibitors are a class of antidepressants that increase the amount of serotonin and norepinephrine in the brain's chemistry. Although it has already proven effective for depression, it can also be used for anxiety and long term nerve pain.

- Khedezla (desvenlafaxine)

- Pristiq (desvenlafaxine succinate)

- Cymbalta (duloxetine)

- Fetzima (levomilnacipran)

- Effexor (venlafaxine)

There are newer medications out on the market now that act like an SSRI but have a boost for serotonin properties as well.

- Trintellix aka Brintellix (vortioxetine)

- Viibryd (vilazodone)

Noradrenergic and serotonergic tetracyclic style antidepressants like Remeron.

The older style tetracyclic antidepressants:

- Elavil

- Tofranil (imipramine)

- Pamelor (nortriptyline)

- Sinequan

Unique pharmaceuticals that are comprised to treat various symptoms like Wellbutrin (bupropion).

Monoamine oxidase inhibitors (MAOI)

- Marplan (isocarboxazid)

- Nardil (phenelzine)

- EMSAM (selegiline)

- Parnate (tranylcypromine)

Commonly prescribed mood stabilization medications

Mood stabilization medications are used in the treatment of mood and depressive disorders like bipolar.

- Carbatrol (carbamazepine)

- Depakote (divalproex sodium)

- Lamictal (lamotrigine)

- Lithium

- Depakene (valproic acid)

- Haldol (haloperidol)

- Loxitane (loxapine)

- Risperdal (risperidone)

- Abilify (aripiprazole)

- Latuda (lurasidone)

There are times when anxiety and sleep problems are combined in the treatment of mood disorders like bipolar. Medications commonly prescribed for this is called a benzodiazepine. These medications have a higher risk of becoming dependent upon and have been known to affect memory.

- Xanax (alprazolam)

- Klonopin (clonazepam)

162

- Valium (diazepam)

- Ativan (Lorazepam)

Like any other pharmaceutical medication, antidepressants and mood stabilizers come at a risk. Side effects for these types of medicines are typical.

- Nausea

- Hair loss

- Weight gain

- Kidney damage

- Pain in the stomach

- Tremors

- Problems with sexual performance or drive

- Liver damage

- Diarrhea

- Skin reactions

Some medications, Depakote, for example, require that the person taking it have blood drawn to check the levels of it in the bloodstream. Too much of it can cause serious problems.

How Do You Know Which Method is Right for You and Your Teenager?

Choosing the herbal route is probably more efficient than choosing the pharmaceutical one. Every circumstance is different though. When deciding if medication, in any form, is going to be the best path for your teenager, it is important to talk to all of the people involved in their care. If your teenager is being considered for pharmaceutical medicine, there is a good chance that there is already a therapist involved. A lot of these medicines, especially the benzodiazepines, are only being prescribed by psychiatrists due to their addictive nature. The prescribing of these have to be considered worth the risk to use them.

Talk to your teenager's therapist and see what other options they might recommend. Maybe there is a new therapy that is being experimented with that they have not tried with your teenager yet. Make sure that your teenager's healthcare provider is up to date on all of the information from the therapist. Most insurance requires that a referral is made to these types of professionals, so there should be some information exchanged between the referring physician and the therapist.

Find an herbalist to talk to. This doesn't mean go to the local vitamin and supplement store and ask the cashier for their opinion on what supplements or herbs would work for your teenager if medication is being recommended. A true herbalist has to have hours upon hours of education and training in order to be considered an herbalist. A lot of times they will have titles following their name because they have to complete a bachelor's degree and a four year Doctor of Naturopathic Medicine program.

At the end of the day, if pharmaceutical medicines are the only means of helping your teenager with their anxiety or depressive disorder, make sure that you are monitoring them closely. Unfortunately, one of the common side effects during the preliminary stage of taking these medications is increased depression or risk of suicide. Have an open line of communication with your teenager while they are taking it so that they can discuss any changes in their mood, health, or feelings. If there are any changes, don't just discontinue using them. Call your teenager's prescribing doctor and find out the right way of stopping the medication. A lot of antidepressants and mood stabilizers cannot just be stopped. They have to be weaned down or else it causes a whole new list of side effects. It is almost like going through withdrawal.

You are the only advocate for your teenager during this time. Their opinion matters, but it is your duty as their parent to make sure that they are safe. If you don't feel like the therapist or the healthcare provider's recommendations are fitting for your teenager, it is okay to request a second opinion. The only time you should go with the gut instinct of the doctors is if your teenager has already attempted suicide or if they are a harm to themselves and others. These types of disorders require swift intervention. Once stable, a course of action can be implemented.

Finding the right medication can be complicated. Everybody's body reacts differently to different medications. Think of it as finding the right fit when buying shoes. Some people have wider feet and require a different width of shoe. Or think about it like getting glasses. Everyone has a different prescription strength. Then there is the option of frames. The option of contacts. Do you get the sunglasses too? The variables in the scenarios are endless. Finding the right medication can feel that way too. It may feel like guesswork most of the time and you will probably become frustrated at the doctor. It is normal. Some people try a handful of different medicines before coming upon the combination that stabilizes them enough to feel slightly normal.

Despite the frustrations, don't take them out on the doctor or your teenager. Neither one of them can tell ahead of time what the right solution is or how the body will react to it. Patience is definitely the primary virtue during this experience.

CONCLUSION

Dealing with an anxiety or depressive at any age is tough. Watching your teenager struggle with it is even harder, especially if they don't want to talk to you about it. Through this book, you have read about all of the different anxiety and depressive disorders that your child or teen could be experiencing. As a parent, it is hard to think about the fact that they could be dealing with something that is so huge. We want to take all of their pain away and fix all of their problems for them. Unfortunately, we don't have that power as parents.

Using this book to learn the signs and symptoms of what might be going on in their head is the first step to helping them. Being able to identify them early on and making an early intervention is the best way to stop something like this from affecting their lives as an adult. It isn't an exact science, and teenagers are teenagers. There is a possibility that they aren't suffering from anxiety or depressive disorders; they are just expressing themselves and rebelling. Hopefully, it is the latter.

If you find yourself at a crossroads, though, trying to figure out what is going on with your child or teen, know that you are not alone. Take a look at yourself and see if you have been repressing your own anxiety and depression. Ask yourself if maybe you have modeled to them that opening up about this isn't acceptable.

There have been great strides made in the mental health community over recent years that make it more acceptable to talk about. Gone are the days where the mentally ill were locked up in asylums and forgot about. As we progress into the future, there needs to be even more acceptance of these disorders. Situational evolution has seemingly forced teenagers and children of younger ages to have to deal with these sorts of disorders and it is out of our control.

The link of genetics that ultimately passes on anxiety and depressive orders to our children is something that can be worked on in the present. It is a chain of events that started within our own family histories for who knows how many years. It is probable that our parents (our teenager's grandparents) suffered from some sort of untreated anxiety or depressive disorder when they were in their early adulthood years, which was then passed on to us (the parent), and so forth. It is up to us to begin breaking this cycle. There is no cure for anxiety or depressive disorders, but there is intervention. There is therapy. There is learning how to cope with things as they get thrown at us. An informed teenager will one day be an informed parent.

There are many kinds of therapy options to explore. We are all different and what works for one person may not work for another. Make sure that you are giving your teenager options. They are less likely to show resistance if they feel like they are part of choosing the treatment plan.

Using exercise as a natural antidepressant is a good first step as well. This is something that you and your teenager can do together. This can also be done at home, so they don't have to worry about you embarrassing them in public when you don your neon spandex and fashionable 90s headband with matching leg warmers. All jokes aside, they will appreciate that you are taking an interest in them.

If there is a chance that your teenager has a rapid onset with their anxiety or depressive disorder, the use of medicine may be imminent. Just make sure that you are looking at all of the options available before you make the final decision. Let them weigh in on it as well. They are the ones who are going through it and they know their body better than anyone else in this world.

Make sure from the very beginning that you are being supportive of your teenager. Make sure that they know none of this is their fault. A lot of times parents feel like it is for attention or that the teenager should be able to control these emotions. Being a teenager is a lot like handling an explosive device. It may be stable and solid from the outside but on the inside one wrong tilt could detonate it. That is what it feels like to be a teenager. Not quite a child, but not quite an adult.

Hopefully, this book has offered you all the answers you seek on helping your teenager, in the instance that it has not, make sure that you are speaking with a licensed professional regarding what your child or teenager is going through. It is okay to ask for help, and when it involves mental illnesses, it is better to ask for help now than to wait and wish you had done it sooner. Choose to cultivate a judgment-free society that can openly discuss mental health. The change starts with you.

* 9 7 9 8 6 0 6 0 8 3 3 7 4 *